Polar Poli Deals of the Century

The US and Russia in the Arctic and Antarctic

Kern Craig

2017

Published by CreateSpace

ISBN-13: 978-1542875905
ISBN-10:   1542875900

Also available on Kindle™

Preface

This book is about polar politics and the biggest deals of the 21st century, deals that will likely be made by President Trump on behalf of the United States and by President Putin of behalf of the Russian Federation. In the meantime, this book serves as the basis for two college courses on polar politics.

Part I is the basis for a course on Arctic affairs. An earlier version of this section was prepared for the annual meeting of the Florida Political Science Association in Lakeland, FL, on April 2, 2016.

Part II is the basis for a course on Antarctic affairs. An earlier version of this section was prepared for the annual meeting of the Florida Political Science Association in Orlando, FL, on April 1, 2017.

Researching and writing this book has taken more than two years. The reference list in the Arctic section contains over 130 sources and the reference list in the Antarctic section contains over 180. There are maps in each section along with numerous hyperlinks.

This book is packed with interesting facts. It has been carefully organized to avoid confusion. Some of the conclusions reached are already controversial. Others are not yet controversial since they are original. But all are defensible in terms of logic and in terms of the evidence presented.

Part I: Arctic Affairs

Kern Craig

Copyright © 2016

This paper was originally prepared as the Arctic Frontier in International Relations for the annual meeting of the Florida Political Science Association in Lakeland, FL, on April 2, 2016.

Abstract

This paper collates scattered information about the Arctic Region in general and the Arctic Ocean in particular. And logical conclusions are drawn given the factual evidence presented. Besides an introduction and conclusion, it consists of seven sections concerning: Arctic Nations, Claims and Agreements, International Law, Pending Claims, Arctic Business, Arctic Pollution, and Arctic Relations. Together this information serves as the basis for a college course on Arctic Affairs.

Introduction

The Arctic Ocean is the smallest, the shallowest, and the coldest of all oceans (Zuhlke, 2016). Yet it has become the center of international attention. The melting of its ice cap is facilitating fishing, drilling, and mining as well as shipping, both destinational (to points within the Arctic) and trans-Arctic. And coastal nations are now extending their claims toward the North Pole not only to promote economic development but also to prevent environmental degradation.

The Arctic is warming twice as fast as the rest of the world. Higher temperature will adversely impact the region in terms of insect infestations as well as forest fires. (Hassol, 2004, p. 10, 14). And greater human activity will increase pollution of the air, water, seabed, and coastline. Entire ecosystems will be affected. This includes the food chain from life on the seabed (the benthos) to invertebrates, fish, marine mammals, and birds (Arctic List, 2013, p. 9).

Arctic warming also poses economic threats particularly in terms of transportation and construction. Shipping will be affected as more icebergs break into the ocean. Trucking will be affected as ice bridges across rivers melt. And building, including the maintenance and construction of airports, will be affected as permafrost melts on land.

Although the perennial ice-pack in the Arctic Ocean is shrinking, first-year winter sea-ice is growing (Melling et al, 2012, p. 105). But it is freezing later and thawing sooner. So there is less sea-ice during the rest of the year. And coastal storms are more destructive when there is less sea-ice to insulate the shoreline (Economist, 2015, p. 36).

The Arctic region is experiencing significant environmental change (Charron, 2015, p. 222). But not all effects of boreal climate change will be negative. Both forests and fish are expected to proliferate in a warmer Arctic. The range of many species, both plants and animals, is projected to shift toward the north on land as well as at sea (Hassol, 2004, p. 10). And most of the economic effects of Arctic warming will be positive not only with respect to forestry and fishing but also with respect to access for shipping, drilling, and mining.

At present the Arctic is sparsely populated with indigenous people and other permanent residents (Broderstad, 2011, p. 893). Natives account for a mere ten percent of the total Arctic population. But they constitute fifty percent in Canada and a large majority in Greenland (Hassol, 2004, p. 6).

Above the Arctic Circle at 66 degrees latitude north, the three largest cities are Russian: Murmansk on the Barents Sea and the inland cities of Vorkuta and Norilsk. But, since the collapse of the Soviet

Union, their populations have decreased by almost a third (Parfitt, 2009). The fourth largest city is Tromso in Norway. It is a vibrant community warmed by waters of the Gulf Stream (Gonorway, 2016). And the people who live in the Arctic obviously have the most to lose and the most to gain from Arctic warming.

Nature (2011) provides three maps depicting the New North at:

http://www.nature.com/news/2011/111012/full/478172a.html

The length of day and night is most extreme at latitude 90 degrees N, the North Pole. The same is true at 90 latitude S, the South Pole. But summer and winter are reversed in the Southern Hemisphere. And the Antarctic and the Arctic are poles apart in other ways as well. Antarctica is land surrounded by water whereas the Arctic is water surrounded by land.

There is also a "polar paradox" since Antarctic land is generally looked upon as international whereas Arctic waters are generally looked up as national. The Antarctic Treaty signed in 1959 "set aside Antarctica as scientific reserve, and suspended all future territorial claims in order to focus on research" (Australian Antarctic

Division, 2015).   But claims to Arctic waters are still being made

under the U.N. Convention on the Law of the Sea signed in 1982.

Arctic Nations

The coastal nations of the Arctic Ocean are known as the Artic 5.

Listed clockwise from the Bering Strait, they are: Russia (with the

longest coastline), Norway (including its Svalbard Archipelago),

Denmark (by virtue of Greenland, the largest island in the world or

the smallest continent after Australia), Canada (including its vast

Arctic archipelago), and the United States (by virtue of Alaska).

The coastline of the Arctic Ocean is 45,389 km (23,203 statute

miles) according to the World Factbook (U.S. Central Intelligence

Agency, 2016). Although it is difficult to measure the coastlines of

the A5 with certainty due to numerous islands and inlets, it is easy to

compare their exposure to the Arctic Ocean using sectors in

approximate degrees of longitude. Russia clearly has the greatest

exposure (160 degrees) followed by Canada (80 degrees), Denmark

with Greenland (60 degrees), Norway with Svalbard (30 degrees),

and the U.S. with Alaska (30 degrees).

"The Arctic sector theory was first publicly propounded by Pascal Porter, a Canadian Senator, in 1907" (Head, 1963, p. 203). He suggested partitioning the Arctic into five sectors extending to the North Pole based upon "the territory of a nation lying immediately below the Arctic Circle." Porter advocated this method as "the most natural" since it was simply "geographical."

"During the Cold War ... the Arctic Ocean (was) portrayed as an 'Arctic Mediterranean' using a novel map projection that placed the Arctic Ocean in the center of the five littoral states ... (but) an expansion of this view to ... a broader set of actors took place after the Cold War" (Keskitalo, 2012, p. 156). The circle of interest widened from the shores of the Arctic Ocean to the Arctic Circle and beyond.

Eight states with territory above the Arctic Circle (including three with no coastline on the Arctic Ocean) have formed the Arctic Council (Brigham, 2014, p. 5). The Arctic 8 includes the Artic 5 plus Finland and Sweden (with land but no water above the Arctic Circle) and Iceland (with water but no land above the Arctic Circle). The Artic Council also includes twelve non-Arctic observers. And it includes nine inter-governmental and inter-parliamentary observer organizations as well as eleven non-governmental observer organizations.

There is talk of an "Arctic landgrab" as the A5 "race to map their claims to a new energy frontier" (Funk, 2009). But "concerns about the growing 'internationalization' of Arctic governance, the potential hidden agendas of non-Arctic states, and the possible dilution of Arctic states' and indigenous peoples' … influence continue to circulate" as well (Lackenbauer, 2014, p. 24). There are "those who tend to view with suspicion the scientific rationale" of observer status given that "fossil fuels … are among the key catalysts for international geopolitical interest" (Chaturvedi, 2014, p. 77, 73). Mining, shipping, and fishing are also factors.

In 2013, South Korea became the first non-Arctic nation to issue an Arctic policy master plan. The South Koreans are interested in shipping and port construction along Russia's Northern Sea Route (Park, 2014, p. 63). Other non-Arctic nations including China, India, Japan, and the Philippines are interested not only in Arctic shipping but also in Arctic fishing (Palosaari, 2012, p. 17).

"The Group of 77 is the largest intergovernmental organization of developing countries in the United Nations, which provides the means for the countries of the South to articulate and promote their collective economic interests" (Group of 77, 2016). And the group is still known as the G-77 even though its membership has now increased to 134 countries constituting a majority of the U.N.'s 193 members (U.N. Department of Public Information, 2016).

These less developed nations, especially the landlocked, are generally opposed to the idea of an Extended Continental Shelf in the Arctic Ocean. The G-77 want the "international seabed to be as large as possible … (since) coastal states are required to make monetary payments or payments in kind through the International Seabed Authority (ISA) for distribution to all state parties to the LOS Convention with respect to the exploitation of nonliving seabed resources" (Riddell-Dixon, 2011, p. 377).

This rent-seeking activity includes all "the seabed and subsoil beyond the limits of national jurisdiction" (International Seabed Authority, 2016). President Reagan opposed such "redistribution of U.S wealth to developing world" and refused to sign the UNCLOS after it was adopted in 1982 due to "its provisions on deep seabed mining" (Heritage Foundation, 2016).

But it is possible that navigation rights in the Arctic Ocean might be even more divisive than resource rights (Dodds, 2013, p. 52). The Arctic 5, meeting in Ilulissat, Greenland, in 2008, issued the Ilulissat Declaration "to position themselves as coastal states who enjoyed … (not only) sovereign rights over exclusive economic zones and outer continental shelves … (but also) the rights of coastal states to … insure higher standards of shipping safety and environmental protection" under Article 234 of the U.N. Convention on the Law of the Sea (2013, p. 50-51).

Article 234 is known as the "Arctic exception" inasmuch as it "recognizes more far-reaching powers for the coastal state than the regimes of innocent and transit passage" (Bartenstein, 2011, p. 23, 45). It "authorizes coastal states to develop and administer special regulations dealing with human activities in ice-covered waters … (and) seeks to upgrade coastal state authority, without abrogating the rights of others to innocent or transit passage" (Arctic Governance Project, 2016).

The Russians already police shipping along their Northern Sea Route and charge "escort fees to international vessels" (Smith and Stephenson, 2013, p. 1192). But the "temporal nature" of Article 234 dealing with "ice covered waters" is currently being debated (Bartenstein, 2011, p. 24, 28, 30). And the argument could become more heated as the ice continues to melt.

The following political map of the Arctic Region, provided by the U.S. Central Intelligence Agency (2012), is found at:

http://www.lib.utexas.edu/maps/islands_oceans_poles/arctic_region_pol_2012.pdf

ARCTIC REGION

Claims and Agreements

In 1825, a treaty between the United Kingdom and Russia established longitude 141 degrees W as their border in North America "in its prolongation as far as the frozen ocean" (Baker and Byers, 2012, p. 71-71) which is now melting!

In 1867, this meridian line was recognized by the United States as the eastern border of Alaska when Alaska was purchased from Russia.

In 1880, it was recognized by Canada when the last Arctic territory was transferred from the United Kingdom.

In 1909, Canadian explorer Bernier deposited a plaque on Melville Island "taking possession for the Dominion of Canada of the whole Arctic Archipelago lying to the north of America from longitude 60 W to 141 W up to latitude 90 N" (Rothwell, 1993, p. 336).

In 1925, Canadian Minister of the Interior, "the Honorable Charles Stewart, told the House of Commons that Canada claimed the territory to the pole" between longitude 60 W and 141 W (Head, 1963, p. 207).

In 1926, the U.S.S.R "formally declared its claim to … territory …
in the Arctic North of the coast of the Union of Soviet Socialist
Republics up to the North Pole" (ibid, p. 206)

In 1945, U.S. President Truman issued Proclamation 2667 that
"extends the U.S. claim to submerged lands and offshore resources
of the Outer Continental Shelf (OCS) in the interest of conservation
and prudent development of the natural resources of the seabed"
(U.S. National Oceanic and Atmospheric Administration, 2009).

In 1945, President Truman also issued Proclamation 2668 that
protects "fishery resources … (with) conservation zones in those
areas of the high seas contiguous to the coasts of the United States"
(Peters and Woolley, 2016).

In 1957, Norway and the Soviet Union agreed on a delimitation line
in the Varangerfjord (Variag Gulf) off the Barents Sea (Tanaka,
2011, p. 461).

In 1958, the United Nations concluded four treaties: the Convention
on the High Seas which took effect in 1962; the Convention on the
Territorial Sea and Contiguous Zone which took effect in 1964; the

Convention on the Continental Shelf which took effect in 1964; and, the Convention on Fishing and Conservation of Living Resources of the High Seas which took effect in 1966 (U.N. Diplomatic Conferences, 2016).

In 1969, Prime Minister Trudeau proclaimed that the Canadian Archipelago "and the waters between the islands and beyond, are looked upon as … national" not international (Rothwell, 1993, p. 338).

In 1970, Canada passed the Arctic Waters Pollution Prevention Act based on "functional sovereignty" with regard to the regulation of tanker traffic given the shortcomings of international law (Bartenstein, 2011, p. 26, 38). The Act extended Canada's jurisdiction 100 nautical miles from the low-water mark along the coast (Rothwell, 1993, p. 339).

In 1970, Canada also extended its territorial sea from three to twelve nautical miles with the Act to Amend the Territorial Sea and Fishing Zones Act. And this encompassed much of the Northwest Passage (ibid).

In 1972, the U.S proclaimed a contiguous zone extending from three to twelve nautical miles offshore (U.S. National Oceanic and Atmospheric Administration, 2016a).

In 1973, Canada and Denmark agreed on a delimitation line between the Canadian archipelago and Greenland (Tanaka, 2011, p. 461).

In 1980, Iceland and Norway agreed on a continental shelf boundary. It was revised by a U.N. Conciliation Commission in 1981 (U.N. Reports of International Arbitral Awards, 1981). And it was revised with an Additional Protocol in 1997 (U.N. Office of Legal Affairs, 2011).

In 1982, the United Nations concluded the Convention on the Law of the Sea replacing the four U.N. treaties of 1958. But the UNCLOS did not become effective until 1994. Implementation was left to other organizations including the International Maritime Organization (IMO), International Whaling Commission (IWC), and International Seabed Authority (ISA) (U.N. Convention on the Law of the Sea, 2013). And enforcement was left to member nations.

In 1983, U.S. President Reagan proclaimed a 200 nautical mile Exclusive Economic Zone (U.S. National Oceanic and Atmospheric Administration, 2016a).

In 1986, "Canada claimed straight baselines around the islands of the Arctic Archipelago" (Rothwell, 1993, p. 331-332). This method was used to increase territorial sea where the coastline was deeply indented (U.N. Convention on the Law of the Sea, 2013). And these straight baselines encompassed the Northwest Passage as "internal waters of Canada over which it had complete sovereignty and jurisdiction" (Rothwell, 1993, p. 344).

In 1988, U.S. President Reagan claimed a 12 nautical mile territorial sea (U.S. National Oceanic and Atmospheric Administration, 2016a).

In 1990, the U.S.S.R. and the U.S. agreed upon their maritime boundary in the North Pacific Ocean, the Bering Sea, the Chukchi Sea, and the Arctic Ocean. They used 168 degrees, 58 minutes, and 37 seconds longitude W as the western limit of Alaskan waters through the Bering Strait "into the Arctic Ocean as far as permitted by international law" (Baker and Byers, 2012, p. 75, 88). This agreement covered territorial seas, exclusive economic zones, and continental shelves (U.S. Department of State, 1990). It was ratified by the U.S. Senate in 1991 but was never ratified by the Russian Parliament.

In 1995, Denmark and Norway agreed to a maritime boundary with respect to Greenland and Jan Mayen Island (between Iceland and the Svalbard Archipelago) (Tanaka, 2011, p. 464).

In 1997, Denmark and Iceland agreed on a maritime boundary delimitation line between Greenland and Iceland (Food and Agriculture Organization of the United Nations, 2016).

In 1999, U.S. President Clinton proclaimed a contiguous zone extending from 12 to 24 nautical miles offshore (U.S. National Oceanic and Atmospheric Administration, 2016a).

In 2001, Russia submitted a claim to the U.N. Commission on the Limits of the Continental Shelf (CLCS) with respect to the Arctic Ocean (U.N. Division for Ocean Affairs and the Law of the Sea, 2015).

The Russian map is found at:

http://www.un.org/depts/los/clcs_new/submissions_files/rus01/RUS_CLCS_01_2001_LOS_2.jpg

In 2006, Norway submitted a claim to the CLCS in respect of the Arctic Ocean (U.N. Division for Ocean Affairs and the Law of the Sea, 2015). The Norwegian claim included the Western Nansen Basin in the Arctic Ocean as well as the Loop Hole in the Barents Sea and the Banana Hole in the Norwegian Sea (U.N. Division for Ocean Affairs and the Law of the Sea, 2009).

In 2006, Denmark and Norway agreed to a maritime boundary with respect to Greenland and the Svalbard Archipelago (Tanaka, 2011, p. 464).

In 2007, the Russians used a submersible craft to plant a Russian flag in 4,261 meters (13,980 feet) of water on the seabed at the North Pole (Derbyshire, 2009). And President Putin indicated that "should be the basis of Russia's position in settling the matter of that part of the Arctic shelf" (Shestak, 2015, p. 170).

In 2010, Norway and Russia signed a treaty on maritime delimitation in the Barents Sea and the Arctic Ocean (Kingdom of Norway, 2010).

In 2013, Denmark submitted a claim to the CLCS with respect to the North-Eastern Continental Shelf of Greenland (U.N. Division for Ocean Affairs and the Law of the Sea, 2015)

In 2014, Denmark submitted a claim to the CLCS with respect to the Northern Continental Shelf of Greenland (ibid).

And, in 2015, Russia submitted a revised claim to the CLCS with respect to the Arctic Ocean (ibid).

International Law

The UNCLOS is fairly straightforward with regard to Territorial Seas, Contiguous Zones, and Exclusive Economic Zones. But it is extremely confusing with regard to Continental Shelves and Extended Continental Shelves (U.N. Convention on the Law of the Sea, 2013).

Territorial Sea (12 NM)

According to Article 2: "The sovereignty of a coastal State extends, beyond its land territory and internal waters and, in the case of an archipelagic State, its archipelagic waters, to an adjacent belt of sea, described as the territorial sea. This sovereignty extends to the air space over the territorial sea as well as to its bed and subsoil."

According to Article 3: "Every State has the right to establish the breadth of its territorial sea up to a limit not exceeding 12 nautical miles (13.8 statute miles or 22.2 kilometers), measured from baselines determined in accordance with this Convention."

According to Article 5: "Except where otherwise provided in this Convention, the normal baseline for measuring the breadth of the territorial sea is the low-water line along the coast as marked on large-scale charts officially recognized by the coastal State."

Contiguous Zone (24 NM)

According to Article 33 (1): "In a zone contiguous to its territorial sea, described as the contiguous zone, the coastal State may exercise the control necessary to: (a) prevent infringement of its customs, fiscal, immigration or sanitary laws and regulations within its territory or territorial sea; (b) punish infringement of the above laws and regulations committed within its territory or territorial sea."

According to Article 33 (2): "The contiguous zone may not extend beyond 24 nautical miles (27.6 statute miles or 44.4 kilometers) from the baselines from which the breadth of the territorial sea is measured."

Exclusive Economic Zone (200 NM)

According to Article 56: "In the exclusive economic zone, the coastal State has: sovereign rights for the purpose of exploring and exploiting, conserving and managing the natural resources, whether living or non-living, of the waters superjacent to the seabed and of the seabed and its subsoil, and with regard to other activities for the economic exploitation and exploration of the zone, such as the production of energy from the water, currents and winds."

According to Article 57: "The exclusive economic zone shall not extend beyond 200 nautical miles (230 statute miles or 370 kilometers) from the baselines from which the breadth of the territorial sea is measured."

Continental Shelf

According to Article 77 (1): "The coastal State exercises over the continental shelf sovereign rights for the purpose of exploring it and exploiting its natural resources."

According to Article 77 (2): "The rights referred to in paragraph 1 are exclusive in the sense that if the coastal State does not explore the continental shelf or exploit its natural resources, no one may undertake these activities without the express consent of the coastal State."

According to Article 77 (3): "The rights of the coastal State over the continental shelf do not depend on occupation, effective or notional, or on any express proclamation."

According to Article 76 (1): "The continental shelf of a coastal State comprises the seabed and subsoil of the submarine areas that extend beyond its territorial sea throughout the natural prolongation of its land territory to the outer edge of the continental margin, or to a distance of 200 nautical miles from the baselines from which the breadth of the territorial sea is measured where the outer edge of the continental margin does not extend up to that distance."

Extended Continental Shelf

The continental shelf beyond 200 nautical miles is known as the Extended Continental Shelf (ECS) or the Outer Continental Shelf (OCS) (Canada Foreign Affairs Trade and Development, 2015b). It is typically measured from the low-tide mark on the shoreline (Gamble, 2009) and is generally "what scientists refer to as the continental margin" (Allain, 2011, p. 14) although "geophysics uses the concept of the 'continental margin' to cover the continental shelf, continental slope, and continental rise" (Koivurova, 2011, p. 214).

According to Article 4 of Annex II, Commission on the Limits of the Continental Shelf: "Where a coastal State intends to establish, in accordance with article 76, the outer limits of its continental shelf beyond 200 nautical miles, it shall submit particulars of such limits to the Commission along with supporting scientific and technical data as soon as possible but in any case within 10 years of the entry into force of this Convention for that State."

According to Article 76 (4) (a): "The coastal State shall establish the outer edge of the continental margin wherever the margin extends beyond 200 M (NM, nautical miles) from the baselines from which the breadth of the territorial sea is measured by either:

(i) a line delineated … by reference to the outermost fixed points at each of which the thickness of sedimentary rocks is at least 1 percent of the shortest distance from such point to the foot of the continental slope; or

(ii) a line delineated … by reference to fixed points not more than 60 M (69 statute miles or 111 kilometers) from the foot of the continental slope."

According to Article 76 (5): "The fixed points … either shall not exceed 350 M (403 statute miles or 648 kilometers) from the baselines from which the breadth of the territorial sea is measured or shall not exceed 100 M (115 statute miles or 185 kilometers) from the 2,500 meter isobath, which is a line connecting the depth of 2,500 meters (8,202 feet)."

According to Article 76 (6): "Notwithstanding the provisions of paragraph 5, on submarine ridges, the outer limit of the continental shelf shall not exceed 350 nautical miles from the baselines from which the breadth of the territorial sea is measured. This paragraph does not apply to submarine elevations that are natural components of the continental margin, such as its plateaux, rises, caps, banks, and spurs."

Based on a submarine elevation claim, a coastal state "can extend its continental shelf beyond what is possible following the 350 nautical mile claim or the 2,500 meters isobaths + 100 nautical miles" (Basaran, 2015, p. 7). And, as previously indicated in Article 76 (1): "The continental shelf of a coastal State comprises ... submarine areas ... throughout the natural prolongation of its land territory." But the UNCLOS is extremely confusing with respect to both the Continental Shelf and the Extended Continental Shelf.

Much is open to interpretation not only about the delimitation of claims but also about the distribution of wealth. According to Article 82: "The coastal State shall make payments or contributions in kind in respect to the exploitation of the non-living resources of the continental shelf beyond 200 nautical miles … annually … after the first five years … for the sixth year, the rate … shall be 1 percent of the value or volume of production … (and) increase by 1 percent for each subsequent year until the twelfth year and shall remain at 7 per cent thereafter … through the Authority, which shall distribute them to States Parties to this Convention."

Pending Claims

"The Eurasian and North American continental margins extend into the deepwater part of the Arctic Ocean" (Laverov et al, 2013, p. 26). And the Arctic Ocean is bisected by the Lomonosov Ridge which extends across the North Pole. Three coastal states have claimed this ridge under Article 76 (1) as a "natural prolongation" of their sovereign territory: Russia, Canada, and Denmark with regard to Greenland (Basaran, 2015, p. 1).

The British Broadcasting Company (BBC) (2014) provides a map showing Arctic claims at http://www.bbc.com/news/world-europe-30481309

Russia made a claim to its northern continental shelf in 2001 and a revised claim in 2015. Denmark made a claim to the northeastern continental shelf of Greenland in 2013 and another to the northern continental shelf of Greenland in 2014 (U.N. Division for Ocean Affairs and the Law of the Sea, 2015). And Canada is still working to define the outer limits of its continental shelf in the Arctic Ocean (Global Affairs Canada, 2015).

Neither Norway nor the United States have a geologic (crustal) basis for extending their territorial waters all the way to the North Pole. But Norway made a claim to a portion of the Arctic Ocean in 2006 (U.N. Division for Ocean Affairs and the Law of the Sea, 2009).

The ongoing boundary disputes among the Arctic 5 include one between Canada and Denmark with respect to the Lincoln Sea and another between Canada and the U.S. with respect to the Beaufort Sea.

There are also differences of opinion between Canada and the U.S. with respect to the Northwest Passage and between Russia and the U.S. with respect to the Northern Sea Route (the Northeast Passage). Generally speaking, the claims of Canada and Russia are based on internal waters and restricted passage whereas the claims of the U.S. are based on international waters and unrestricted passage.

But, by in large, "these disagreements are well-managed and pose no sovereignty or defense challenges" (Government of Canada, 2015a, p. 13). And the same can be said about the dispute between Russia and the United States over their maritime boundary from the North Pacific Ocean and the Bering Sea to the Chukchi Sea and the Arctic Ocean. It was settled de facto if not de jure in 1990.

No U.S. claims have been made under the U.N. Convention on the Law of the Sea since President Regan refused to sign the treaty in 1982 and since the Senate refused to ratify the revised treaty signed by President Clinton in 1994. The U.S. can however "rely upon customary international practice to obtain many of the benefits of these treaties without subjecting itself to the risks of joining them" (Meese, Spring, and Schaefer, 2007). And it "will be in an advantageous position compared to the other Arctic states, as it will not subject its assertion of the outer limit of the U.S. continental shelf to the scrutiny" of the U.N. Commission on the Limits of the Continental Shelf (Golitsyn, 2009, p. 405).

The United States is cooperating with the other members of the Arctic 5 to meet challenges from outside the region. Outsiders want a slice of the Arctic pie. And their emphasis will likely be on the exploitation rather than the stewardship of natural resources. So it is in the interest of the A5 to regulate access. And such regulation is possible if the A5 act in concert.

"Since the Arctic Ocean is a relatively shallow basin "compared with the Earth's other oceans … about 90 percent will ultimately be carved up" by coastal nations (Funk, 2009). "Only the deep basins on either side of the disputed Lomonosov Ridge are likely to remain part of the Arctic Ocean Commons" (Gamble, 2009).

Claims to extended continental shelves by the A5 under Article 76 depend on one of "three parameters: the shape of the seabed, the depth of the water, and the thickness of the underlying sedimentary material" (MacNab, 2004, p. 3). But Russia and Canada also use straight baselines, as do over eighty other nations, to extend claims along their coastlines (Pedrozo, 2011, 494-496). And this method encompasses Russia's North Sea Route and Canada's Northwest Passage.

According to Article 7 of the UNCLOS: "In localities where the coastline is deeply indented and cut into, or if there is a fringe of islands along the coast in its immediate vicinity, the method of straight baselines joining appropriate points may be employed in drawing the baseline from which the breadth of the territorial sea is measured." And this like many other articles in the UNCLOS is open to considerable interpretation.

The International Boundaries Research Unit (2015) provides a map of "Maritime jurisdiction and boundaries in the Arctic region" at https://www.dur.ac.uk/ibru/resources/arctic/

Arctic Business

Fishing

Canada, Denmark, Norway, Russia, and the United States held a Meeting on Arctic Fisheries in Nuuk, Greenland, in 2014. The Arctic 5 concluded that "commercial fishing in the high seas of the central Arctic Ocean is unlikely to occur in the near future … (but) agreed on the desirability of developing interim measures to deter unregulated fishing" (Pew Charitable Trusts, 2014).

The "accord would regulate commercial harvests … in the so-called doughnut hole of the Arctic Ocean … international water that includes the North Pole and is encircled by the exclusive economic zones of the coastal countries" (Kramer, 2015, May 19). It is an exceptional agreement given not only its preemptive nature but also given the ongoing disputes with Russia regarding Crimea, Ukraine, and Syria.

Shipping

"The Arctic Ocean is distinctive from the world's other oceans in that … there is only one major high seas point of access" (Rothwell, 2012, p. 271). This is West of Russia through the Norwegian and Greenland Seas and is referred to as the Barents Sea Opening or less accurately as the Barents Strait (O'Dwyer, Kasajima, & Nost, 2001).

Chokepoints to the Atlantic Ocean include the Fram Strait between the Svalbard Archipelago (Norway) and Greenland (Denmark), the Denmark Strait between Iceland and Greenland, the Davis Strait between Greenland and Baffin Island (Canada), and the Nares Strait between Greenland and Ellesmere Island (Canada).

West of Alaska (the U.S.) and East of Siberia (Russia), there is a single route from the Arctic Ocean to the Pacific Ocean: the Bering Strait. It is only 53 nautical miles wide (61 statute miles or 98 kilometers) (Rothwell, 2012, p. 272). And it is choked with ice flows for two-thirds of the year (Ricci, 2012).

"The points of access to the Arctic Ocean are through different bodies of water, all of which are referred to as straits but which have varying legal status under the law of the sea … (and) Part III of the LOS Convention, titled 'Straits Used for International Navigation' … suggests both a geographical and functional element" (Rothwell, 2012, p. 270).

So it is not surprising that Arctic coastal nations interpret the LOS differently. And the United States, even though not a party to the Convention, nevertheless remains a straitlaced advocate of both "innocent passage" and "transit passage" as set forth in its Freedom of Navigation Program of 1979 (Oral, 2012). But, as with adolescence, the rights of passage should be tempered with the responsibilities of safe passage. And according to Article 19 (1) of the UNCLOS: "Passage is innocent so long as it is not prejudicial to the peace, good order or security of the coastal State."

The Arctic Ocean is also distinctive from the world's other oceans in terms of its two southern shipping routes: the Northwest Passage through Canadian waters and the Northern Sea Route through Russian waters. And, despite much evidence to the contrary, the U.S. maintains that both the NWP and the NSR are "international waters" (Charron, 2006, p. 45).

The NWP through the Canadian Archipelago includes numerous straits including the narrow McClure Strait (East of the Beaufort Sea between Melville Island to the North and Banks Island to the South). It is only 37 nautical miles wide (43 statute mile or 69 kilometers). And it is choked with ice year round (Martin, 2010, p. 58). Furthermore, there is "no dispute over Canada's ownership and title to the islands of the Canadian Arctic Archipelago" (Rothwell, 1993, p. 333-334).

The NSR along the Russian Coast "passes through some straits which are less than 10 meters deep" (Kendrick, 2014). And the parts suitable for navigation lie in "the internal sea waters, the territorial sea and the exclusive economic zone of the Russian Federation" (Northern Sea Route Information Office, 2016).

Section 8 of Article 234 of the United Nations Convention on the Law of the Sea already permits "coastal states … to adopt and enforce non-discriminatory laws and regulations for the prevention, reduction, and control of marine pollution from vessels in ice-covered areas within the limits of the exclusive economic zone" 200 nautical miles from shore (Arctic Governance Project, 2016).

"Shipping lanes must be determined and speed and staggering requirements set in order to minimize shipping's footprint in this vital ecosystem" (Lajeunesse, 2012, p. 529). And local pilots must be employed not only at ports but throughout the Arctic Ocean to prevent collisions with icebergs broken off from ice shelves and glaciers as well as with "bergy bits" or "growlers" broken off from icebergs (U.S. National Oceanic and Atmospheric Administration, 2014).

Drilling and Mining

"The Arctic holds an estimated 13% … of the world's undiscovered conventional oil resources and 30% of its undiscovered conventional natural gas resources, according to the U.S. Geological Survey" (U.S. Energy Information Administration, 2012). And "apart from oil and gas, the Arctic abounds in other mineral resources, including diamonds, gold, silver, tin, iron ore, zinc, uranium, and nickel" (Ruel, 2011, p. 827).

Although "the Arctic Ocean centers on an area of 'high seas' … that falls outside all national boundaries" (New Scientist, 2009), the high seas are relatively small part of a relatively small and shallow ocean. The Arctic Ocean is 15.6 million square kilometers (6.0 million square miles) (U.S. National Oceanic and Atmospheric Administration, 2016b). But only 2.8 million square kilometers (1.1 million square miles), roughly 18 percent, are beyond Exclusive Economic Zones (Pew Charitable Trusts, 2016).

The "donut hole" may not be all that important anyway. The area of central high seas holds less promise in terms of fishing, drilling, and mining than areas closer to shore. "No more than five percent of the natural resources are to be found outside the exclusive economic zones … of one or another Arctic state" (Ruel, 2011, p. 827). And access to the donut hole through the waters of littoral nations will no doubt be restricted.

Roughly fifty percent of the floor of the Arctic Ocean is continental shelf (the highest percentage of any ocean). The remainder is interrupted by three submarine ridges: the Alpha Cordillera (group), the Nansen Cordillera (group), and the Lomonosov Ridge (U.S. Central Intelligence Agency, 2015). And coastal nations are now extending their national boundaries based on the shape and composition of the seabed as well as the depth of the ocean.

"Russia … lays claim to the largest portion of the Arctic … (and) the right to defend the territory with its military might" (Ostrow, 2013, p. 57-58). Canada could claim the second largest based on its northern exposure followed by Denmark (including Greenland), Norway (including Svalbard), and the United States (including Alaska). And sector claims of the five coastal nations would converge at the North Pole.

If most or all of the Arctic Ocean is claimed by the Arctic 5, fishing and shipping could be regulated, policed, and taxed to maximize safety, minimize pollution, and prevent over-fishing of endangered species. This could be done on any basis, e.g., the type and tonnage of the catch as well as the route, tonnage, and seaworthiness of the vessel.

Similarly, mining and drilling could be regulated, policed, and taxed to maximize safety, minimize pollution, and prevent under-reporting of actual production. And this could also be done on any basis, e.g., blocks of territory leased as well as royalties on resources extracted.

Both private companies and state owned enterprises could be thoroughly vetted before entering the Arctic Ocean. And, even if they are deemed to be both operationally and financially sound, third-party performance bonds and liability insurance could be required. In addition, wilderness areas could be set aside to prohibit some or all business activity.

Such action on the part of the Arctic 5 is preferable to any "existing civil liability regime established globally" (Ebinger, Banks, and Schackmann, 2014, p. 39). It would be easier to obtain an actionable consensus among the coastal nations than among the United Nations. A regional regime would also be stricter in terms of regulation and enforcement. And it would be better funded. In all of these respects, the track record of the U.N. is less than stellar.

Arctic Pollution

Global pollution is affecting the Arctic Region. But the emission of pollutants is declining in North America and Europe whereas it is increasing in eastern and southern Asia (Law et al, 2014). The U.N. needs to implement its Environmental Program by establishing one "speed limit" for all "drivers" as opposed to double standards. "In the name of universal progress as well as equal treatment, all nations should be held accountable for both their actions and their inactions" (Craig, 2011, p. 48).

Modeling indicates that "rerouting most cross-polar aircraft flights around the Arctic Circle … increased fuel use and total pollution emissions by 0.56%, but … also reduced emissions within the Arctic Circle by 83%, and … the reduction in pollutants, particularly black carbon … decreased Arctic and global temperatures and Artic sea ice loss" (Jacobson et al, 2012, p. 723). The U.N. should therefore consider rewriting the "rules of the road" through the International Civil Aviation Organization (ICAO) and enforcing them UNiformly (sic).

If the U.N. is not up to the task, one should expect coastal nations to act unilaterally or cooperatively based on the precautionary principle. This could be accomplished in conjunction with Air Defense Identification Zones. Although ADIZs exist beyond sovereign territory, they operate in the interest of national security. And "such a concept has never been challenged as being inconsistent with existing law" (Abeyratne, 2011).

Due to rapid loss of sea ice, it is becoming possible for ships to circumnavigate the Arctic Ocean during the summer. The NSR shortens the distance from East Asia to Western Europe by 8,200 kilometers (4,428 nautical miles) compared to the Suez Canal. And the NWP shortens the distance by 10,400 kilometers (5,616 nautical miles) compared to the Panama Canal (Rodrigue, 2016).

Arctic sea routes save both time and fuel but shipping increases the risk of environmental contamination whether from deliberate dumping or accidental sinking. The International Maritime

Organization has adopted a Polar Code but its "regulations depend on flag state enforcement" (Wanerman, 2015, p. 437). And enforcement may be particularly lax if it is based on third-party flags of convenience.

In order to fly their planes, sail their ships, and drive their trucks and cars, the people of the world have made a Faustian bargain to sell their souls to the devil of pollution. Regionally, this manifests itself as the "Arctic paradox" since the combustion of hydrocarbons contributes to Artic warming which facilitates the production of Arctic hydrocarbons (Palosaari, 2012, p. 24). And the United Nations will have as much trouble dealing with this dilemma in the Arctic as it has dealing with the devil in the rest of the world.

Given the shortcomings of the U.N., it is up to the Arctic 5 to regulate traffic across the region as well as fishing, drilling, and mining. Arctic nations have the most to lose if other nations exploit Arctic resources for economic benefit without regard to environmental cost. Many nations have signed regional trade agreements such as the North American Free Trade Agreement due to the shortcomings of the World Trade Organization. Likewise, many coastal nations should sign regional security agreements to protect their coastal waters. And, if the Artic 5 act in unison, they have the wherewithal to both minimize pollution and maximize production. But that is a big if.

Mercury is an especially dangerous pollutant for people and other animals in the Arctic due to their mostly marine diet. "Asia is the major anthropogenic source ... and this is independent of the climate" (Hansen, Christensen, and Brandt, 2015, p. 11254). Most of the mercury is going into the Arctic Ocean via Russian rivers: the Lena, the Ob, and the Yenisei. It is evidently "runoff from gold, silver, and mercury mines in Siberia" (Harvard School of Public Health, 2012).

The bi-products of atomic energy are also dangerous. The 1996 Protocol to the London Convention of 1972 (the Convention on the Prevention of Marine Pollution by Dumping of Wastes and Other Matter), "represents a major change of approach to the question of how to regulate the use of the sea as a depository for waste materials in that, in essence, dumping is prohibited, except for materials on an approved list" (International Maritime Organization, 2016b). Since radioactive waste is omitted, it is prohibited. But it still may be dumped covertly. And, once dumped, it remains radioactive for "hundreds of thousands of years" (Greenpeace, 2015). Unfortunately, neither Russia nor the United States "support any discussion of nuclear contamination in the Arctic" (Pedersen, 2012, p. 149).

"From 1946 through 1993, thirteen nuclear capable countries used the ocean ... to dispose of nuclear/radioactive waste ... (and) the United States alone dumped vast quantities of nuclear material off its coasts between 1946 and 1970" (Kozakiewicz, 2014). After the collapse of the Soviet Union in 1992, the Russians admitted to the disposal of radioactive waste in the Arctic Ocean. The Yablokov Report of 1993 indicated that sixteen reactors from nuclear vessels were dumped in the adjacent Kara Sea. But three reprocessing plants in Western Europe (one in France and two in the United Kingdom) dumped even more "radwaste" in the Atlantic Ocean. And it was transported to the Arctic Ocean via the Gulf Steam (Krupnick, 2001, p. 35).

Arctic Relations

Arctic 2

"For the entire length of the Cold War, the Arctic Ocean remained a critically important and dangerous theater of operation" (Huebert, 2011, p. 818). The world was bipolar not only in terms of its North and South Poles but also in terms of its east and west superpowers, the U.S.S.R. and the U.S., both coastal states of the Arctic Ocean.

So what has changed? Russians and Americans still play war games of cat and mouse with planes above the ice, ships around the ice, and submarines below the ice. And because of mutually assured destruction (MAD), they continue to avoid nuclear war as well as any other form of direct military conflict. But many other nations now have the capability to operate militarily in the Arctic.

Although secrecy still prevails, one should expect to see greater cooperation between Russia and the United States: first, to discourage any foreign military operations including terrorism; and, second, to regulate all foreign commercial operations especially those involving environmental pollution and resource extraction.

"Based on a series of reports suggesting that more ice will melt ... (it is safe to) assume that more vessels will venture into the Arctic, resulting in more threats" (Charron, 2015, p. 219-220).

Greater cooperation between Russia and America is also probable as the two become more and more alike. In terms of political economy, the former is becoming more capitalist and the latter more socialist. And joint measures in defense of Arctic waters can now be expected since both countries share diminished status as declining super-powers and face not only increased competition from rising super-powers such as China and India but also increased terrorism from jihadists.

It is however important to remember that both Russia and the United States are still nuclear superpowers. There are five nuclear-weapon states (NWS) officially recognized in the Nonproliferation Treaty (NPT). The United Kingdom has 120 strategic warheads, China 260, and France 300 whereas Russia has 1,582 and the United States 1,597 (Arms Control Association, 2015).

Russia and the United States are clearly capable of dealing with external threats to the Arctic region. And they "are closely cooperating in the framework of the Arctic Council" (Seliverstova, 2015). Any conflict between the two over oil and gas beneath the Arctic Ocean seems unlikely. The region is "divided into thirds with one-third onshore, one-third continental shelf, and one-third deep ocean basin … (and) the deep ocean basin areas - areas over which there are border disagreements - contain few hydrocarbon resources" (Johnston, 2012, p. 23).

Arctic 3

As temperature rises and ice melts, the Arctic Ocean is "enmeshed increasingly in high politics … a fact that has led some to call for cooperation among Canada, Russia, and the United States" – the A3 (Young, 2012, p. 171). Russia has by far the longest Arctic coastline followed by Canada with its extensive archipelago (Pedersen, 2012, p. 148). Together, they account for three-quarters of the total (Bonikowsky, 2012) or two-thirds using the sector method. And, although the U.S. has only Alaska, the U.S is still an economic and military superpower.

Arctic 5

The Arctic 5 includes the A3 plus the other littoral nations, Denmark and Norway. And the claims of these five states are based on land, both shoreline and seabed, whereas the claims of all other nations are based on water. The A5 clearly have the most coastal "skin in the game" economically, environmentally, and militarily. So "there is a dichotomy of interests in the Arctic Ocean" between adjacent nations asserting their rights to regulate access in territorial waters, exclusive economic zones, and extended continental shelves versus distant nations asserting their rights of open access through international straits and high seas (Berkman, 2012, p. 150-151).

The A5 have nonetheless "adhered to the LOS Convention … to draw the outer limits of their continental shelves … (given) extensive flexibility in the LOS Convention regarding those limits … (and given) there will not be much ocean floor … left for the ISA (International Seabed Authority) to administer in the Arctic Ocean" (Koivurova, 2011, p. 217). "The Arctic is an unusual Ocean in that shelves shallower than 500 m (1,640 feet) underlie more than half of its area" (Melling et al, 2012, p. 97). And Article 76 (5) of the

UNCLOS extends territorial sea 100 nautical miles (115 statute miles or 185 kilometers) beyond the 2,500 m isobaths, a line connecting points 2,500 meters (8,202 feet) deep.

"Whether one views increased development in the Arctic as an opportunity, a threat or both, there will be a need for sustainable and coordinated management by Arctic countries" (Arctic Alliance, 2015). There is "no need to develop a new comprehensive legal regime to govern the Arctic Ocean" given the existing framework of cooperative management among the five littoral nations (Arctic Ocean Conference, 2008). But the A5 may wish to consider a more formal arrangement such as an Arctic Treaty Organization (ATO) along the lines of the North Atlantic Treaty Organization (NATO).

In 2008, the Arctic 5 adopted the Ilulissat Declaration emphasizing their "sovereign rights" under international law including the "national implementation ... of relevant provisions." They also acknowledged their "stewardship role" in the Arctic Ocean and indicated their willingness to "work together ... through bilateral and multilateral arrangements" (OceanLaw, 2008).

In 2015, the A5 "taking a precautionary approach" signed a Declaration Concerning the Prevention of Unregulated High Seas Fishing in the Central Arctic Ocean (U.S. Department of State, 2015b). They stressed that the "high seas" of the Arctic Ocean are "entirely surrounded by waters under the fisheries jurisdiction of Canada, the Kingdom of Denmark in respect of Greenland, the Kingdom of Norway, the Russian Federation and the United States of America" (Government of Norway, 2015).

Geographic proximity is also a crucial factor in emergency response. And "Arctic states … employ … port state control arrangements that have … potential to impose costly responses to rule violations" (Stokke, 2013, p. 81). The Arctic 5 have a greater ability as well as a greater interest when it comes to governing Arctic waters than any other international organization whether regional or global.

Membership in the Artic 5 is limited to the littoral nations of the Arctic Ocean. "Denmark's Arctic credentials would thus be challenged if … Greenland were to … opt for full independence" (Lunde, 2014, p. 41). And the same could be said about the United

States if Alaska were to secede. But that is even less likely than the secession of Svalbard from Norway.

Denmark granted self-governance to Greenland in 2009 although political matters relating to foreign policy and national defense are shared between the two. And "in the Arctic Council, it is Denmark who officially has a seat at the table, but in practice it is Greenland who is most active" (Smits, van Tatenhove, and van Leeuwen, 2014, p. 341). It may not be a marriage based on love but it is one based on convenience since Demark has the money and Greenland has the land.

Arctic 8

Three other nations with territory above the Arctic Circle collaborate with the A5 in the Arctic Council: Finland, Sweden, and Iceland (U.S. Department of State, 2015a). Together they are known as the Arctic 8. Although "the council is … precluded from addressing issues related to security … this leaves open three major areas that touch on both economics and the environment: fishing, mining, and oil drilling" (Wanerman, 2015, 449-450).

"Finland had a small stretch of shore on the Arctic Ocean in Petsamo but … that area was lost to the Soviet Union" after World War II (Lankinen, 2013). "Sweden does not have an Arctic coastline … (and) only a small portion of its northern region lies above the Arctic Circle" (Bonikowsky, 2012). The island of "Iceland is a small and marginal player … in the Arctic region … (and) resides just south of the Arctic Circle" (Lunde, 2014, p. 42).

Other more distant states participate to a lesser extent in the Arctic Council. Six nations were added as observers in 2013 (UArtic, 2015) bringing the total to twelve: France, Germany, Netherlands, Poland, Spain, United Kingdom, China, Italy, Japan, South Korea, Singapore, and India (Arctic Council, 2015b).

"Russia along with Canada, was apparently among the leading states behind the 'Observer Manual' … (that) spelled out limitations on financial contributions and levels of participation" in the Arctic Council (Zysk, 2014, p. 33). And, given the length of their Arctic coastlines, Russian and Canadian interest in limiting the influence of non-Arctic nations is hardly surprising.

"A unique feature of the Arctic Council is the involvement of six international Indigenous peoples' organizations as Permanent Participants" (Canada Foreign Affairs Trade and Development, 2015a): The Aleut International Association, Arctic Athabaskan Council, Inuit Circumpolar Council, Gwich'in Council International, Russian Association of Indigenous Peoples of the North, and the Saami Council.

In 2011, the Arctic Council reached an Agreement on Cooperation on Aeronautical and Maritime Search and Rescue in the Arctic. The scope of SAR extends north from the shorelines of the A5, across the Arctic Ocean, all the way to the North Pole. But "the delimitation of search and rescue regions is not related to … any boundary between states or their sovereignty" (Arctic Portal, 2011).

In 2013, the Arctic Council adopted an Agreement on Marine Oil Pollution Preparedness and Response in the Arctic. And each of the eight states agreed to "undertake monitoring activities in order to identify oil pollution incidents in areas under its jurisdiction and, to the extent possible, in adjacent areas beyond the jurisdiction of any state" (U.S. Department of State, 2013).

The Arctic Council also created the Arctic Economic Council which met for the first time in 2014 (Arctic Economic Council, 2016). The AEC is organized as an "independent forum of business representatives to … promote responsible economic development" (Arctic Council, 2015a). It is designed to facilitate "Arctic-to-Arctic business opportunities, trade, and investment in the North, which will ultimately benefit Northern families and communities" (Government of Canada, 2015b).

In 2014, the U.S. Secretary of State appointed a Special Representative for the Arctic. And, in 2015, "the United States assumed the two-year rotating chairmanship of the Arctic Council" (U.S. Department of State, 2015d). U.S. priorities included search and rescue operations, marine protected areas, ocean acidification, and oil pollution in the Arctic Ocean and the impact of pollution from outside the Arctic especially soot (black carbon) and methane.

The United States organized a conference on Global Leadership in the Arctic: Cooperation, Innovation, Engagement, and Resilience. GLACIER brought together the foreign ministers of Arctic nations and other interested parties. This happened during the U.S.

Chairmanship of the Arctic Council but was not a Council sponsored event (U.S. Department of State, 2015c). The focus of the conference was not only on the impact of global climate change in the North but also on the impact of Arctic climate change in the South.

The Arctic 8 are acting in "a concerted manner in the International Maritime Organization (IMO) to convert the nonbinding … Polar Code … to a legally binding one … to protect the Arctic marine environment from shipping" pollution even where vessels have rights of innocent passage under the Law of the Sea (Koivurova, 2012, p. 138-139). The focus of both the Arctic Council and the IMO is on "Safe Arctic Shipping" (ShipArc, 2015). And the Polar Code which becomes effective in 2017 (International Maritime Organization, 2016a) builds upon the Council's "enactment of a search and rescue agreement" in 2011 (Wanerman, 2015, p. 431).

Nongovernmental organizations also contribute their expertise. The Artic Research Consortium of the U.S. is a nonprofit organization of "educational and scientific institutions that have a substantial commitment to arctic research … (and it) pairs K-12 teachers with researchers" (ARCUS, 2015). And the International Arctic Science Committee is an NGO that encourages and facilitates cooperation by "all countries engaged in Arctic research" (International Arctic Science Committee, 2016).

But outside interest is a two way street. It could result in a loss of focus or even a reversal of focus if the interests of non-Arctic nations take precedence. This happened with both the EU and NATO as they became involved with nations in the Middle East and Southwest Asia.

Conclusion

"The oceans once belonged to everyone and to no one … (and) freedom of the seas served the world well for ages. But this anarchic principle is now hopelessly inadequate given the present environmental crisis involving massive water pollution and widespread extinction of marine species" (Craig, 2010a, p. 15).

"The ocean's resources, a single ecosystem, which transcend artificially created national boundaries, require a management system" (Epstein, 2011, p. 762). But what system? Perhaps the choice is between global capitalism and global socialism, between private property and public property, between market freedom and government control? If a single global system is not desirable or possible then perhaps the choice is between regional, national, or local systems.

Overall, there seem to be three main possibilities with respect to oceanic regimes. Two are global in scope although both are based on national interest. Richer countries tend to favor capitalism with its emphasis on production whereas poorer countries tend to favor socialism with its emphasis on distribution. But neither greater production nor wider distribution lessens the tragedy of the oceanic commons.

The third possibility is national in scope and based on national interest. Yet it operates regionally and serves globally. Coastal countries tend to favor the extension of territorial waters. But, since they are opposed by landlocked countries, they tend to collaborate with their coastal neighbors. And, since they have more to gain from aqua-enterprise and more to lose from marine pollution, they tend to favor both economic production and environmental protection.

The Artic 5, being more developed nations, face opposition from less developed nations. This is not however an insurmountable problem. America and Russia are old superpowers. The two new superpowers, India and China, have extensive coastlines of their own to exploit and protect. And they are distracted by their own border disputes over land.

India is far more concerned about the activities of China and Pakistan in the Indian Ocean than about the activities of the A5. And India is not only traditionally aligned with Russia, it is also newly aligned with America. India is also becoming more capitalistic and democratic, richer and freer. Its government is thus becoming more preoccupied with consumers and voters at home.

China is far more concerned about waters of the Yellow Sea, East China Sea, and South China Sea than about waters of the Arctic Ocean. Chinese "decision-making processes … remain obscure" (Jakobson and Peng, 2012, p. 22). But "because China is a staunch proponent of the need to respect sovereignty, it will not question the mineral and territorial rights of the Arctic states" (Hallgren, 2012).

The extension of territorial waters by the littoral nations of the Arctic Ocean will be the best way to promote economic development and insure environmental protection in the short term. In the long run, "deconstruction of the nation-state" and "disaggregation of the mixed political economy" will be even better (Craig, 2010b, p. 414).

Eventually government power will shift upwards to macro-regional levels and global organizations as socialist uniformity and regulation are used to alleviate the pollution of both water and air. And eventually market power will shift downwards to micro-regional levels and local governments as capitalist diversity and freedom are used to alleviate the poverty of landlubbers.

But, in the meantime, neither the United Nations nor the indigenous population is up to the task of simultaneously exploiting and protecting the Arctic Ocean. It is therefore up to coastal nations to extend their sovereign rights over territorial seas, contiguous zones, exclusive economic zones, continental shelves, outer continental shelves, and contiguous high seas.

Regional economic opportunities will stimulate cooperative economic enterprise including fishing, shipping, drilling, and mining. And regional environmental threats will stimulate cooperative environmental stewardship. The Arctic 5 have the proximate incentive as well as the immediate ability to simultaneously exploit and protect the waters and seabed of the Arctic Ocean. They also have an opportunity to develop "best practices" that will serve as good examples in other regions of the world.

References

Abeyratne, R. (2011). In search of theoretical justification for air defense identification zones. *Journal of Transportation Security*, September 2001. DOI 10.1007/s12198-011-0083-2

Allain, M.A. (2011). Canada's claim to the Arctic: A study in overlapping claims to the outer continental shelf. *Journal of Maritime Law and Commerce*, 42, 1, 1-47.

Arctic Alliance (2015). *Governance: Issue brief.* http://www.arcticalliance.net/governance.cfm

Arctic Council (2015a). *News release: Arctic Council renews commitment to Arctic economic and social development and environmental protection.* http://www.arctic-council.org/index.php/en/events/meetings-overview/ministerial-meeting-2015/1040-news-release-arctic-council-renews-commitment-to-arctic-economic-and-social-development-and-environmental-protection-5

Arctic Council (2015b). *Observers.* http://www.arctic-council.org/index.php/en/about-us/arctic-council/observers

Arctic Economic Council (2016). *Backgrounder*.

http://arcticeconomiccouncil.com/about-us/backgrounder/

Arctic Governance Project (2016). *UNCLOS Article 234.*

http://www.arcticgovernance.org/unclos-article-234.4668244-

142904.html

Arctic List (2013). Mapping Arctic dialogue: Past & upcoming

events (2012-2013). *Artic Yearbook.*

http://www.google.com/url?sa=t&rct=j&q=&esrc=s&source=

web&cd=4&ved=0CDMQFjADahUKEwj58_rEoMnHAhWD

DJIKHdqhBAM&url=http%3A%2F%2Fwww.arcticyearbook.

com%2Ffiles%2Fthearcticlist.pdf&ei=PAHfVfnlI4OZyATaw5

IY&usg=AFQjCNFC4ZCTMsOqt-NGv07UgHDd2abKRg

Arctic Ocean Conference (2008). *Ilulissat Declaration.* Ilulissat,

Greenland: Arctic Governance Project.

http://www.arcticgovernance.org/the-ilulissat-

declaration.4872424.html

Arctic Portal (2011). *Agreement on Cooperation on Aeronautical and Maritime Search and Rescue in the Arctic.* http://library.arcticportal.org/1874/1/Arctic_SAR_Agreement_EN_FINAL_for_signature_21-Apr-2011%20(1).pdf

ARCUS (2015). *About us.* Fairbanks, AK: Arctic Research Consortium of the United States. file:///C:/Users/KWC/Downloads/arcus_brochure.pdf

Arms Control Association (2015). *Nuclear weapons: Who Has What at a Glance.* https://www.armscontrol.org/factsheets/Nuclearweaponswhohaswhat

Australian Antarctic Division (2015). *Who owns Antarctica?* http://www.antarctica.gov.au/about-antarctica/people-in-antarctica/who-owns-antarctica

Baker, J.S, & Byers, M. (2012). Crossed lines: The curious case of the Beaufort Sea maritime boundary dispute. *Ocean Development and International Law,* 43, 1, 70-95.

Bartenstein, K. (2011). The "Arctic Exception" in the Law of the Sea Convention: A contribution to safer navigation in the Northwest Passage? *Ocean Development & International Law*, 42, 1/2, 22-52.

Basaran, I. (2015). The Lomonosov Ridge and the overlapping outer continental shelf claim to North Pole. *Journal of Maritime Law and Commerce*, 46, 1, 1-21.

Berkman, P. (2012). Geopolitics of Arctic sea-ice minima. *Brown Journal of World Affairs*, 19, 1, 145-153.

Bonikowsky, L.N. (2012). The Arctic, country by country. *Diplomat & International Canada*.
http://diplomatonline.com/mag/2012/10/the-arctic-country-by-country/

Brigham, L. (2014). The changing Arctic: New realities and players at the top of the world. *Asia Policy*, 18, 5-13.

British Broadcasting Company (2014). *Denmark challenges Russia and Canada over North Pole*.
http://www.bbc.com/news/world-europe-30481309

Broderstad, E. G. (2011). The promises and challenges of indigenous self-determination. *International Journal*, 66, 4, 893-907.

Canada Foreign Affairs Trade and Development (2015a). *The Arctic Council.* http://www.international.gc.ca/arctic-arctique/council-conseil.aspx?lang=eng

Canada Foreign Affairs Trade and Development (2015b). *Canada's extended continental shelf.* http://www.international.gc.ca/arctic-arctique/continental/index.aspx?lang=eng

Charron, A. (2006). The Northwest Passage in context. *Canadian Military Journal*, Winter 2005-2006. http://www.journal.forces.gc.ca/vo6/no4/north-nord-02-eng.asp

Charron, A. (2015). Canada, the Arctic, and NORAD: Status quo or new ball game. *International Journal*, 70, 2, 215-231.

Chaturvedi, S. (2014). India's Arctic Engagement: Challenges and opportunities. *Asia Policy*, 18, 73-79.

Craig, K. (2010a). The extension of territorial waters. *US-China Law Review*, 7, 5, 15-25.

Craig, K. (2010b). The new world order: A deconstruction of the nation-state and a disaggregation of the mixed-political-economy. *International Journal of Public Administration*, 33(8-9), 414-420.

Craig, K. (2011). The blame game in international relations. *National Social Science Journal*, 35, 2, 43-55.

Derbyshire, E. (2009). *Geographic North Pole*. http://gigapan.com/gigapans/7626/

Dodds, K. (2013). The Ilulissat Declaration (2008): The Arctic States, "Law of the Sea," and Arctic Ocean. *SAIS Review*, XXXIII, 2, 45-55.

Ebinger, C., Banks, J.P., & Schackmann, A. (2014). *Offshore oil and gas governance in the Arctic: A leadership role for the U.S. Brookings Energy Security Initiative*. http://www.google.com/url?sa=t&rct=j&q=&esrc=s&source=web&cd=3&ved=0CCwQFjACahUKEwj58_rEoMnHAhWDD JIKHdqhBAM&url=http%3A%2F%2Fwww.brookings.edu%2 F~%2Fmedia%2FResearch%2FFiles%2FReports%2F2014%2

F03%2Foffshore-oil-gas-governance-arctic%2FOffshore-Oil-

and-Gas-Governance-

web.pdf%3Fla%3Den&ei=PAHfVfnlI4OZyATaw5IY&usg=A

FQjCNGlXcWRsGOjHqbBwak8qCI-sqGAFg

Economist (2015, September 5). *Arctic America: Tales of Atlantis.*

http://www.economist.com/news/united-states/21663265-

presidents-visit-arctic-will-not-prevent-villages-sliding-sea-

tales

Epstein, A. (2011). A new approach to an old problem: Managing

fish resources in the Beaufort Sea. *Chicago Journal of

International Law,* 11, 2, 755-787.

Food and Agriculture Organization of the United Nations (2016).

FAOLEX-Legislative database of FAO Legal Office.

http://faolex.fao.org/cgi-

bin/faolex.exe?rec_id=016869&database=FAOLEX&search_t

ype=link&table=result&lang=eng&format_name=@ERALL

Funk, M. (2009). Arctic landgrab. *National Geographic,* 215, 5,

104-121.

Gamble, J. (2009). Arctic landgrab. *Scientific American*, 301, 2, L4-L9.

Global Affairs Canada (2015). *Canada's Extended Continental Shelf*. http://www.international.gc.ca/arctic-arctique/continental/index.aspx?lang=eng

Golitsyn, V. (2009). Continental shelf claims in the Arctic Ocean: A commentary. *International Journal of Marine & Coastal Law*, 24,2, 401-408.

Gonorway (2016). *Tromso*. http://www.gonorway.no/norway/counties/troms/tromsoe/7636 48d5fc445c0/index.html

Government of Canada (2015a). *Canada's northern strategy: Our north, our heritage, our future*. http://www.northernstrategy.gc.ca/cns/cns.pdf

Government of Canada (2015b). *IQALUIT 2015: Development for people of the north*. http://www.international.gc.ca/arctic-arctique/assets/pdfs/aclb-eng.pdf

Government of Norway (2015). *Arctic Fisheries Declaration.*

https://www.regjeringen.no/globalassets/departementene/ud/ve

dlegg/folkerett/declaration-on-arctic-fisheries-16-july-2015.pdf

Greenpeace (2015). *1993 – Dumping of radioactive waste at sea gets*

banned.

http://www.greenpeace.org/international/en/about/history/Vict

ories-timeline/radioactive-dumping/

Group of 77 (2016). *Establishment, Aims, Structure, Finance,*

Activities. http://www.g77.org/doc/

Hallgren, J. (2012). Preface. In L. Jakobson, & J. Ping, *China's*

Arctic aspirations: SIPRI Policy Paper No. 34. Solna, Sweden:

Stockholm International Peace Research Institute.

http://books.sipri.org/product_info?c_product_id=449

Hansen, K.M., Christensen, J.H., & Brandt, J. (2015). The influence

of climate change on atmospheric deposition of mercury in the

Arctic – A model sensitivity study. *International Journal of*

Environmental Research and Public Health, 12, 11254-11268.

Harvard School of Public Health (2012). *Toxic mercury, accumulating in the Arctic, springs from a hidden source.* http://www.hsph.harvard.edu/news/press-releases/arctic-rivers-toxic-mercury/

Hassol, S.J. (2004). *Impacts of a Warming Arctic.* Cambridge: Cambridge University Press. http://www.amap.no/documents/doc/impacts-of-a-warming-arctic-2004/786

Head, I.L. (1963). Sovereignty in the Arctic regions. McGill Law Journal, 9, 3, 200-226.

Heritage Foundation (2016). *Why the "Law of the Sea Treaty" is still a bad idea.* http://heritageaction.com/stoplost/why-the-law-of-the-sea-treaty-is-still-a-bad-idea/

Huebert, R. (2011). Submarines, oil tankers, and icebreakers. *International Journal,* 66, 4, 809-824.

International Arctic Science Committee (2016). *About IASC.* http://iasc.info/iasc/about-iasc

International Boundaries Research Unit (2015). *Arctic Maritime Jurisdiction Map*. Durham University, UK: Centre for Borders Research. https://www.dur.ac.uk/ibru/resources/arctic/

International Maritime Organization (2016a). *Shipping in Polar Waters*. http://www.imo.org/en/MediaCentre/HotTopics/polar/Pages/default.aspx

International Maritime Organization (2016b). *The 1996 Protocol to the Convention on the Prevention of Marine Pollution by Dumping of Wastes and Other Matter, 1972*. http://www.imo.org/en/OurWork/environment/pollutionprevention/pages/1996-protocol-to-the-convention-on-the-prevention-of-marine-pollution-by-dumping-of-wastes-and-other-matter,-1972.aspx

International Seabed Authority (2016). *The Mining Code*. https://www.isa.org.jm/mining-code

Jacobson, M.Z., Wilkerson, J.T., Balasubramanian, S., Cooper, W.W., & Mohleji, N. (2012). The effects of rerouting aircraft around the arctic circle on arctic and global climate. *Climate Change*, 115, 709-724.

Jakobson, L., & Ping, J. (2012). *China's Arctic aspirations: SIPRI Policy Paper No. 34*. Solna, Sweden: Stockholm International Peace Research Institute. http://books.sipri.org/product_info?c_product_id=449

Johnston, P. (2012). Arctic energy resources: Security and Environmental Implications. *Journal of Strategic Security*, 5, 3, 13-32.

Kendrick, L. (2014). Map shortcomings could hinder Northern Sea Route Growth. *Barents Observer*. http://barentsobserver.com/en/arctic/2014/06/map-shortcomings-could-hinder-northern-sea-route-growth-28-06

Keskitalo, E.C. (2012). Setting the agenda on the Arctic: Whose policy frames the region? *Brown Journal of World Affairs*, XIX, I, 155-164.

Kingdom of Norway (2010). *Treaty on maritime delimitation and cooperation in the Barents Sea and the Arctic Ocean signed today.* https://www.regjeringen.no/en/aktuelt/treaty/id614254/

Koivurova, T. (2011). The actions of the Arctic states respecting the continental shelf: A reflective essay. *Ocean Development & International Law*, 42, 211-226.

Koivurova, T. (2012). The Arctic Council: A testing ground for new international environmental governance. *Brown Journal of World Affairs*, XIX, I, 131-144.

Kozakiewicz, P. (2014). *The disposal of nuclear waste into the world's oceans.* http://www.cbrneportal.com/the-disposal-of-nuclear-waste-into-the-worlds-oceans/

Kramer, A.E. (2015). Russia and U.S. Find Common Cause in Arctic Pact. *New York Times, May 19, 2015.* http://www.nytimes.com/2015/05/20/world/russia-and-us-find-common-cause-in-arctic-pact.html

Krupnick, C. (2001). *Decommissioned Russian Nuclear Submarines and International Cooperation*. Jefferson, NC: McFarland and Co.

Lackenbauer, P.W. (2014). Canada and the Asian observers to the Arctic Council: Anxiety and opportunity. *Asia Policy*, 18, 22-29.

Lajeunesse, A. (2012). A new Mediterranean? Arctic shipping prospects for the 21st century. *Journal of Maritime Law and Commerce*, 43, 4, 521-537.

Lankinen, T. (2013). *Finland left out of the Arctic Ocean*. Tampere University Press. http://researchandstudy.uta.fi/2013/03/12/finland-left-out-of-the-arctic-ocean/

Laverov, N.P., Lobkovsky, L.I., Kononov, M.V., Dobretsov, N.L., Vernikovsky, V,A., et al. (2013). Geodynamic model of the evolution of the Arctic basin and adjacent territories in the Mesozoic and Cenozoic and the outer limit of the Russian continental shelf. *Geoctonics*, 47, 1, 1-30.

Law, K.S., Stohl, A., Quinn, P.K., Brock, C.A., Burkhart, J.F., Paris, J., Ancellet, G., Singh, H.B., Roiger, A., Schlager, H., Dibb, J., Jacob, D.J., Arnold, S.R., Pelon, J., & Thomas, J.L. (2014). Arctic air pollution: New insights from Polarcar-IPY. *Bulletin of the American Meteorological Society*, 95, 12, 1873-1895.

Lunde, L. (2014). The Nordic embrace: Why the Nordic countries welcome Asia to the Arctic table. *Asia Policy*, 18, 39-45.

MacNab, R. (2004). The case for transparency in the delimitation of the outer continental shelf in accordance with UNCLOS Article 76. *Ocean Development and International Law*, 35, 1, 1-17.

Martin, A.G.L. (2010). International Straits: Concept, Classification and Rules of Passage. Berlin: Springer.

Meese, E., Spring, B., & Schaefer, B.D. (2007). *The United Nations Convention on the Law of the Sea: The Risks Outweigh the Benefits.*
http://www.heritage.org/research/reports/2007/05/the-united-nations-convention-on-the-law-of-the-sea-the-risks-outweigh-the-benefits

Melling, H., Francois, R., Myers, P.G., Perrie, W., Rochon, A., & Taylor, R.L. (2012). The Arctic Ocean: A Canadian perspective from IPY. *Climate Change*, 115, 89-113.

Nature (2011). Redrawing the Arctic map: The new north. *Nature*, 478, 7368, 172-173.
http://www.nature.com/news/2011/111012/full/478172a.html

New Scientist (2009). Rules of high seas could lead to Arctic 'pole or peace'. *New Scientist*, 202, 2711, 6.

Northern Sea Route Information Office (2016). *NSR*.
http://www.arctic-lio.com/NSR

OceanLaw (2008). *Ilulissat Declaration*. Ilulissat, Greenland: Arctic

Ocean Conference.

http://www.oceanlaw.org/downloads/arctic/Ilulissat_Declaratio

n.pdf

O'Dwyer, J., Kasajima, Y., & Nost, O.A. (2001). North Atlantic

Water in the Barents Sea Opening, 1997-1999. *Polar Research*,

20, 2, 209-216.

http://brage.bibsys.no/xmlui/bitstream/handle/11250/174262/O

DwyerPR2001.pdf?sequence=1

Oral, N. (2012). *Transit Passage Rights in the Strait of Hormuz and*

Iran's Threats to Block the Passage of Oil Tankers.

https://www.asil.org/insights/volume/16/issue/16/transit-

passage-rights-strait-hormuz-and-iran%E2%80%99s-threats-

block-passage

Ostrow, R. (2013). Pax Russia: Russia's role in the race for the

Arctic. *SAIS Review*, XXXIII, 2, 57-59.

Parfitt, T. (2009). In from the cold: Workers flee Stalin's frozen north before the lights go out. *The Guardian*, February 22, 2009. http://www.theguardian.com/world/2009/feb/23/russia-mining

Park, Y.K. (2014). South Korea's interests in the Arctic. *Asia Policy*, 18, 59-65.

Palosaari, T. (2012). The amazing race: on resources, conflict, and cooperation in the Arctic. *Nordia Geographical Publications*, 40(4), 13-30. http://tampub.uta.fi/handle/10024/67984

Pedersen, T. (2012). Debates over the role of the Arctic Council. *Ocean Development & International Law,* 43, 2, 146-156.

Pedrozo, R. (2011). A response to Cartner's and Gold's commentary on "Is it time for the United States to join the Law of the Sea?" *Journal of Maritime Law and Commerce,* 42, 4, 487-510.

Peters, G., & Woolley, J.T. (2016). *Proclamation 2668 (of September 28, 1945), Policy of the United States with Respect to Coastal Fisheries in Certain Areas of the High Seas.* http://www.presidency.ucsb.edu/ws/?pid=58816

Pew Charitable Trusts (2014). *Meeting on Arctic Fisheries. Nuuk, Greenland, February 24-26, 2014.* http://www.pewtrusts.org/~/media/assets/2014/09/arcticnations agreetoworkoninternationalfisheries-accord.pdf?la=en

Pew Charitable Trusts (2016). *Why an International Fisheries Agreement Is Needed in the Central Arctic Ocean.* http://www.pewtrusts.org/en/projects/arctic-ocean-international/solutions/faqs

Riddell-Dixon, E. (2011). Meeting the deadline: Canada's Arctic submission to the Commission on the Limits of the Continental Shelf. *Ocean Development & International Law*, 42, 4, 368-382.

Ricci, T. (2012). *Connecting two continents: The ultimate engineering challenge.* American Society of Mechanical Engineers. https://www.asme.org/engineering-topics/articles/arctic-engineering/connecting-two-continents-the-ultimate-engineering

Rodrigue, J.P. (2016). The Geography of Transport Systems. https://people.hofstra.edu/geotrans/eng/ch1en/conc1en/polarroutes.html

Rothwell, D.R. (1993). The Canadian-U.S. Northwest passage dispute: A reassessment. *Cornell International Law Journal*, 26, 2, 331-372. http://scholarship.law.cornell.edu/cgi/viewcontent.cgi?article=1309&context=cilj

Rothwell, D.R. (2012). International straits and trans-Arctic navigation. *Ocean Development and International Law*, 43, 3, 267-282.

Ruel, G.K. (2011). The Artic show must go on. *International Journal*, 66, 4, 825-833.

Seliverstova, N. (2015). *US, Russia cooperate on Arctic issues.* http://arctic.ru/international/20151204/248728.html

Shestak, O.I. (2015). Basic directions and mechanisms of state policy in Arctic and development of the Arctic Zone of the

Russian Federation (2000-2014). *Asian Social Science*, 11, 19, 168-177.

ShipArc (2015). *Arctic Council International Conference on Safe and Sustainable Shipping in a Changing Arctic Environment.* Malmo, Sweden: World Maritime University. http://wmu.se/events/shiparc-2015

Smith, L.C. & Stephenson, S.R. (2013). New trans-Arctic shipping routes navigable by midcentury. *National Academy of Sciences*, E1191-E1165. http://www.pnas.org/content/110/13/E1191.full

Smits, C.C.A., Tatenhove, J.P.M., & Leeuwen, J. (2014). Authority in Arctic governance: Changings spheres of authority in Greenlandic offshore oil and gas developments. *International Environmental Agreements*, 14, 329-348.

Stokke, O.S. (2013). Regime interplay in Arctic shipping governance: Explaining regional niche selection. *International Environmental Agreements*, 13, 65-85.

Tanaka, Y. (2011). Reflections of Arctic maritime delimitations: A comparative analysis between the case law and state practice. *Nordic Journal of International Law*, 80, 4, 459-484.

UArtic (2015). *Networking with non-Arctic organizations: New partnerships for new friendships.* University of the Arctic. http://www.uarctic.org/news/2015/9/networking-with-non-arctic-organizations-new-partnerships-for-new-friendships/

U.N. Convention on the Law of the Sea (2013). *UNCLOS.* http://www.un.org/depts/los/convention_agreements/texts/unclos/unclos_e.pdf

U.N. Department of Public Information (2016). *General Assembly of the United Nations.* http://www.un.org/en/ga/

U.N. Diplomatic Conferences (2016). *United Nations Conference on the Law of the Sea, 1958.* http://legal.un.org/diplomaticconferences/lawofthesea-1958/lawofthesea-1958.html

U.N. Division for Ocean Affairs and the Law of the Sea (2009). *Commission on the Limits of the Continental Shelf (CLCS):*

Outer limits of the continental shelf beyond 200 nautical miles from the baselines: Submissions to the Commission: Submission by the Kingdom of Norway. http://www.un.org/Depts/los/clcs_new/submissions_files/subm ission_nor.htm

U.N. Division for Ocean Affairs and the Law of the Sea (2015). *Submissions, through the Secretary-General of the United Nations, to the Commission on the Limits of the Continental Shelf, pursuant to article 76, paragraph 8, of the United Nations Convention on the Law of the Sea of 10 December 1982.* http://www.un.org/depts/los/clcs_new/commission_submission s.htm

U.N. Office of Legal Affairs (2011). *Submission in Compliance with the Deposit Obligations Pursuant to the United Nations Convention on the Law of the Sea.* http://www.un.org/depts/los/LEGISLATIONANDTREATIES/ STATEFILES/NOR.htm

U.N. Reports of International Arbitral Awards (1981). *Conciliation Commission on the Continental Shelf area between Iceland and Jan Mayen: Report and recommendations to the governments of Iceland and Norway, decision of June 1981.* http://legal.un.org/riaa/cases/vol_XXVII/1-34.pdf

U.S. Central Intelligence Agency (2012). *Arctic region (political map).* http://www.lib.utexas.edu/maps/islands_oceans_poles/arctic_region_pol_2012.pdf

U.S. Central Intelligence Agency (2015). Arctic Ocean. *World Factbook.* https://www.cia.gov/library/publications/the-world-factbook/geos/xq.html

U.S. Central Intelligence Agency (2016). *Coastline.* https://www.cia.gov/library/publications/the-world-factbook/fields/2060.html

U.S. Department of State (1990). *Agreement with the Union of Soviet Socialist Republics on the Maritime Boundary.* http://www.state.gov/e/oes/ocns/opa/c28187.htm

U.S. Department of State (2013). *Agreement on Cooperation on Maritime Oil Pollution Preparedness and Response in the Arctic.* http://www.state.gov/r/pa/prs/ps/2013/05/209406.htm

U.S. Department of State (2015a). *The Arctic Council.* http://www.state.gov/e/oes/ocns/opa/arc/ac/

U.S. Department of State (2015b). *Arctic Nations Sign Declaration to Prevent Unregulated Fishing in the Central Arctic Ocean.* http://www.state.gov/r/pa/prs/ps/2015/07/244969.htm

U.S. Department of State (2015c). *Conference on Global Leadership in the Arctic: August 30-31, 2015.* http://www.state.gov/e/oes/glacier/index.htm

U.S. Department of State (2015d). *U.S. Chairmanship of the Arctic Council.* http://www.state.gov/e/oes/ocns/opa/arc/uschair/index.htm

U.S. Energy Information Administration (2012). Arctic oil and natural gas resources. *Today in Energy.* https://www.eia.gov/todayinenergy/detail.cfm?id=4650

U.S. National Oceanic and Atmospheric Administration (2009). *Proclamation 2667 of September 28, 1945, Policy of the United States with Respect to the Natural Resources of the Subsoil and Sea Bed of the Continental Shelf.* http://www.gc.noaa.gov/documents/gcil_proc_2667.pdf

U.S. National Oceanic and Atmospheric Administration (2014). *National Ocean Service.* http://oceanservice.noaa.gov/facts/iceberg.html

U.S. National Aeronautics and Space Administration (2016a). *Maritime zones and boundaries.* http://www.gc.noaa.gov/gcil_maritime.html

U.S. National Oceanic and Atmospheric Administration (2016b). *Arctic Theme page.* http://www.arctic.noaa.gov/faq.html

Wanerman, R.O.G. (2015). Freezing out non-compliant ships: Why the Arctic Council must enforce the Polar Code. *Case Western Reserve Journal of International Law*, 47, 429-451.

Young, O. (2012). Arctic politics in an era of global change. *Brown Journal of World Affairs*, XIX, I, 165-178.

Zuhlke, S. (2016). The Arctic Ocean. *National Geographic Society*.

http://education.nationalgeographic.org/media/arctic-ocean/

Zysk, K. (2014). Asian interests in the Arctic: Risks and gains for

Russia. *Asia Policy*, 18, 30-38.

Part II: Antarctic Affairs

Kern Craig

This paper was originally prepared as the Antarctic Frontier in International Relations for the annual meeting of the Florida Political Science Association in Orlando, FL, on April 1, 2017.

Abstract

This paper collates scattered information about the continent of Antarctica and the surrounding Southern Ocean. Logical conclusions are then drawn from the factual evidence presented. Besides an introduction and conclusion, it consists of eight sections: Antarctic Exploration, Territorial Claims, Regional Agreements, International Law, Unsettled Disputes and Pending Claims, Science and Business, Climate Change, and Antarctic Relations. Together this information serves as the basis for a college course on Antarctic Affairs.

Introduction

As the Last Continent to be discovered, "academics have been rather late in discovering Antarctica (Beck, 1986, p. 7). "Remarkably, the 2007 Encyclopedia of the Antarctic ... has no section on Antarctic politics or governance" (Brady, 2013, p. 3). "Security discourse, a familiar narrative in the context of regions such as the Middle East and the Arctic, is much less frequently engaged in with respect to the Antarctic" (Hemmings, Rothwell, and Scott, 2012). This paper serves to partially fill that void in the literature.

A simplified Map of Antarctica showing surrounding oceans and regional seas is shown on the next page (National Snow & Ice Data Center, 2016b). A more detailed physical map can be found at the website of Nations Online Project (2016):

http://www.nationsonline.org/oneworld/map/antarctica_map.htm

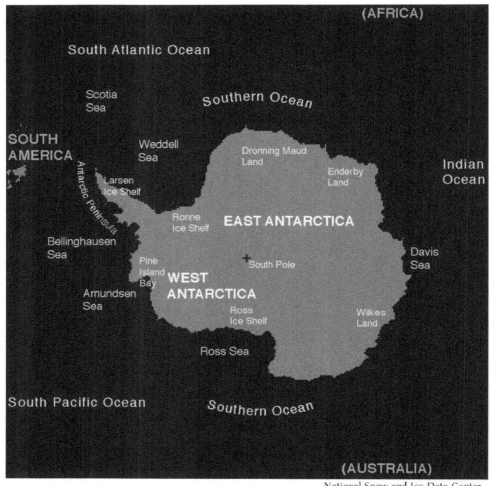

National Snow and Ice Data Center

Antarctica is the fifth largest of the world's seven continents, larger than Europe and larger than Australia and New Zealand combined (Antarctic Geological Drilling, 2016). Antarctica is unique. On average, it is the coldest, driest, and highest continent on earth (Howard, 2013, p. 13). It is also the windiest (Masson-Delmotte, 2013, p. 77) and the stormiest. The average barometric pressure is the lowest on earth. And giant cyclones circle around the continent (Berkman, 2002, p. 48).

The record speed for down-slope, katabatic, wind across East Antarctica is 327 km per hour (Fahrbach, 2013, p. 140). Wind speed greater than 160 km per hour is common (National Research Council, 2011, p. 119). And winds over 100 km per hour can blow for days (Australian Antarctic Division, 2016a). The combination of strong wind and dry air generate enormous amounts of static electricity (Rubin, 2008, p. 305).

Antarctica averages 2250 m above sea level (Rubin, 2008, p. 92) and it is drier in the higher regions. Most precipitation is in the form of snow and average accumulation is equivalent to 150 mm of rain per year. On the coast it is more than 200 mm per year with the highest, over 2000 mm, next to the Bellingshausen Sea (on the west side of the Antarctic Peninsula). On the elevated plateau it is less than 50 mm (Australian Antarctic Division, 2016a). Although the amount of snowfall per year is relatively low, its accumulation over millions of years has resulted in an enormous amount of ice (Antarctic Geologic Drilling, 2016).

Antarctica is essentially a desert but almost all of the continent is covered with ice (Cassano, 2013, p. 135, 102). Even during the months of summer, less than 1.0% of the surface is ice-free. The ice-free area is relatively small but it includes the 3000 square km of the three main Dry Valleys: Victoria, Wright, and Taylor (Rubin, 2008, p. 288).

During the middle of winter, Antarctica is extremely cold and totally dark. Temperatures less than -50°C are common (National Research Council, 2011, p. 119). The Antarctic Circle at 66°33′ S, like the Arctic Circle at 66°33′ N, marks the latitude where the sun remains below the horizon on Midwinter's Day and above the horizon on Midsummer's Day. But, in Antarctica, June marks the middle of winter and December marks the middle of summer (Australian Antarctic Division, 2016d).

These seasonal differences are due to the tilt of the earth's axis. And, since it varies from year to year, the latitude of the Polar Circles is based on an average tilt of 23.5° (using 23°67' the latitude is 90° - 23°67' = 66°33'). Although seasons are reversed between southern and northern hemispheres, periods of winter darkness and summer lightness increase as one moves closer to either pole. If not for the tilt, there would be continuous night at both poles and uniform cycles of day and night elsewhere (Berkman, 2002, p. 8). As it is, both poles remain dark for almost half of the year and light for almost half (Joyner, 1998, p. 9).

Antarctica has the highest average elevation of any continent, more than 2,000 m, twice as high as the next highest continent, Asia (Antarctic Geologic Drilling, 2016). Mountain peaks, known as nunataks, protrude through the icecap especially along the periphery of Antarctica. But, unlike other continents, Antarctica has low seismic activity and few active volcanoes (Storey, 2013, p. 42).

Most of the hot spots are in the vicinity of the Antarctic Peninsula, West Antarctica, and the Ross Sea. In these regions, there is a high probability of significant eruptions. Mt. Erebus on Ross Island is 3794 m high and "one of only a handful of volcanoes in the world with a permanent convecting-lava lake" (Rubin, 2008, p. 298, 300).

In the northwest, there are mountains all along the Antarctic Peninsula. The rest of the continent is divided into West and East Antarctica at 0° and 180° of longitude, the prime meridian (or Greenwich Meridian) and the anti-meridian (or International Date Line). West Antarctica is known as Lesser Antarctica whereas East Antarctica is known as Greater Antarctica since most of the continent is located in the eastern hemisphere.

The Transantarctic Mountains, 2900 km long, separate the older part of the continent, East Antarctica, from the newer part, West Antarctica (Rubin, 2008, p. 92, 302). The highest mountains, the Ellsworth Mountains, are positioned in the opposite direction and are located in West Antarctica along with a number of other small ranges (Storey, 2013, p. 37-38). And the highest peak, Vinson

Massif at 4900 m, is located in the Ellsworth Mountains (Rubin, 2008, p. 73).

The Gamburtsev Mountains are in the lowlands of East Antarctica. But they are 600 m beneath the surface of an ice sheet that is 4 km thick. The lowest point on the continent is located in the Bentley Subglacial Trench in Marie Byrd Land but it is under the deepest ice on the continent. And, at -2,540 m below sea level, it is the lowest elevation on the planet that is not under seawater (U.S. Central Intelligence Agency, 2016a).

There are also over 300 freshwater lakes beneath the ice including Lake Vostok, the largest at 50 km wide, 250 km long, and over 300 m deep (Storey, 2013, 38, 40-41). And the icecap above the lake is at least 3.6 km thick (Convey, Brandt, and Nicol, 2013, p. 201). Numerous topographic maps of Antarctica produced by the U.S. Geological Survey can be found at the U.S. Antarctic Resource Center (2016): http://usarc.usgs.gov/drg_dload.shtml

The ice and land mass of Antarctica is nearly 14 million square km, roughly 1.4 times larger than the United States (National Research Council, 2011, p. 18, 71) or about 10% of the earth's surface

(Joyner, 1998, p. 3). Even in the summertime, less than 0.4% of the continent is ice-free (Convey, Brandt, and Nicol, 2013, p. 161). But that is approximately 44,890 square km, roughly the size of Denmark (Rubin, 2008, p. 26), although new research indicates that the ice-free portion is only .18% (Phys.org, 2016).

The area of permanent snow and ice is huge, more than 13 million square km (Masson-Delmotte, 2013, p. 67). It is not only bigger than the continent of Australia, it is almost the size of South America. And, in some places, this extraordinary accumulation of snow and ice is up to 4.5 km thick (Rodgers, 2013, p. 301). The water frozen in Antarctica represents about 80% of the world's terrestrial freshwater (Masson-Delmotte, 2013, p. 77).

The land-based East Antarctic ice sheet consists of a dense sheet of ice over a solid mass of land (Joyner, 1998, p. 3) whereas the marine-based West Antarctic Ice Sheet consists mainly of ice shelves floating on the ocean (Joyner, 2013, p. 116). Parts of the WAIS are more than 1.7 km below sea (Convey, 2010). Ice shelves originating from the edges of ice sheets surround approximately half of the continent. They extend 100 or so km from their grounding lines and are anywhere from 200 to 700 m thick (National Research Council, 2011, p. 55).

Icebergs calve from Antarctica's glaciers, ice sheets, and ice shelves (National Snow & Ice Data Center (2016c) (2016d). And hundreds of thousands float in the Southern Ocean. They range in size from tiny growlers and small bergy bits to gigantic icebergs more than 100 km long. The largest extend 40 m above the surface and 300 m below (Rubin, 2008, p. 93). In 2002, an entire ice shelf the size of Rhode Island, the Larsen B, crumbled into the ocean off the eastern Antarctic coast (Conway, 2010).

Glaciers, ice sheets, ice shelves, and icebergs originate on land and consist of frozen freshwater whereas sea ice originates in the ocean and consists of frozen salt water (National Snow & Ice Data Center, 2016a). There are three types of sea ice: fast ice, frozen fast to the continent; drift ice, floating loosely in the ocean; and, pack ice, floating but tightly consolidated (Historical Sea Ice Atlas, 2016). Sea ice of one kind or another surrounds most of Antarctica. In the winter, it extends as far as 55° S (in some places up to 1500 km from shore) (National Research Council, 2011, p. 45, 51).

Sea ice floating in the northern Weddell Sea and the southern Ross Sea increases from 3 million square km in the summer to 18 million in the winter. And this temporarily doubles the area of Antarctica covered by ice (Masson-Delmotte, 2013, p. 69). This is why Antarctica is sometimes called the Pulsating Continent (Beck, 1986, p. 9). And "as sea ice crystallizes salt is squeezed out" making the Southern or Austral Ocean not only the coldest but also the saltiest and the densest of all oceans (Masson-Delmotte, 2013, p. 75).

Cold saline water sinks under warm fresh water due to the difference in densities. This exchange of water is facilitated by the narrow and deep continental shelf that surrounds most of the continent. Antarctic Bottom Water is the primary source of abyssal circulation (Berkman, 2002, p. 106-108). Water from the margins of Antarctica drive "the circulation of currents across all the oceans" (Convey, 2014, p. 1).

The Antarctic coastline is 17,968 km (U.S. Central Intelligence Agency, 2016b). The Antarctic Circumpolar Current (ACC) flows clockwise around the continent from west to east. It is the largest current on the planet with a width of 100 to 200 km and a depth of approximately 4 km. And gale force winds are possible 20% of the time in the Screaming Sixties (around 60° S) (Australian Antarctic Division, 2016e)

40° S roughly corresponds to the northern extent of the Southern Ocean where the water is warmer and fresher. This is the transition zone between subantarctic waters and subtropical waters. "Defined in this way, the Southern Ocean occupies about 20% of the surface of the global ocean" (Australian Antarctic Division, 2016e). The area of the Southern Ocean is estimated at 20.3 million square km with an average depth of 4500 m and a maximum depth of 7235 m (Fahrback, 2013, 137, 140, 148). And, during the winter, it is mostly covered with sea ice one to three meters thick.

The entire Ross Ice Shelf is floating in the sea. It covers an area of roughly 520,000 square km, about the size of France. Toward the continent, it is up to 1000 m thick but toward the ocean is less than 100 m thick. Like other ice shelves, it is constantly increasing in size on land because of snowing and decreasing in size at sea because of melting. In 1987, the Ross Ice Shelf calved an iceberg

(B-15) measuring 37 km by 298 km, the world's largest, larger than the island of Jamaica (Rubin, 2008, p. 301).

As part of the Southern Ocean, there are a number of seas surrounding the continent of Antarctica. Listed clockwise, they are: the Lazarev Sea just east of 0° longitude, the Riiser-Larsen Sea at 25° E, the Cosmonauts Sea at 40° E, the Cooperation Sea (also known as the Commonwealth Sea) at 70 ° E, the Davis Sea at 90° E, the Mawson Sea at 110° E, the D'Urville Sea at 140° E, Somov Sea at 160° E, the Ross Sea at 180°, the Amundsen Sea at 110° W, the Bellingshausen Sea (on the west side of the Antarctic Peninsula) at 90° W, the Scotia Sea at 60° W (at the tip of the Antarctic Peninsula), the Weddell Sea (on the east side of the Antarctic Peninsula) at 40° W, and the King Haakon VII Sea just west of 0°.

These locations are only approximate and there are disputes over nomenclature as well as boundaries. It should also be noted that the Ross Sea and the Waddell Sea resemble huge bays more than seas. Refer to the detailed International Bathometric Chart of the Southern Ocean (IBCSO, 2016):

http://hs.pangaea.de/Maps/bathy/IBCSO_v1/IBCSO_v1_digital_chart_pdfA.pdf

Under the ice shelf in the Waddell Sea, 79° S is the most southerly point in the Southern Ocean. But it is still over 2000 km from 90° S, the South Geographic Pole (Convey, Brandt, and Nicol, 2013, p. 182). And, when speaking of Antarctic poles, it should be noted there are a total of five.

The Geographic Pole, or Geodetic Pole, at 90° S marks one end of the earth's rotational axis where lines of longitude converge. It is currently located near the U.S. station Amundsen-Scott. This is the spot where "all time zones coexist … where days intersect and it is possible to move forward into yesterday or backward into tomorrow before running into today" (Berkman, 2002, p. 7). But, due to a slight wobbling of the earth, the Geographic Pole is moving at about 10 km per annum in the direction of 43° W (Rubin, 2008, p. 327).

The Pole of Inaccessibility, or Relative Inaccessibility, at 83° S, 55° E marks the spot farthest in every direction from the coast. It is approximately 870 km from the Geographic Pole.

The Geomagnetic Pole is currently at 78° 30′ S, 111° E near the Russian station Vostok roughly 1283 km from the Geographic Pole. It is a dipole at the intersection of the surface of the earth and the axis of a bar magnet at the center of the earth marking a theoretical point at the southernmost end of the earth's geomagnetic field (Stackexchange.com, 2017).

The Pole of Cold is also near the Russian station Vostok. The record for the lowest temperature on the surface of the earth, -89.2°C, was recorded there in 1983 (Australian Antarctic Division, 2016a).

Last but not least, the Magnetic Pole currently at 64.5° S, 137.7° E, marks the spot where lines of force converge upward, the point away from which all compass needles point (Sitwell, 2009). It is roughly 2858 km from the Geographic Pole. But, due to changes in the earth's magnetic field, the Magnetic Pole is moving in a north to northwesterly direction at 5 km per annum. Currently, it is located in the French sector of the Southern Ocean beyond the Antarctic Circle (Australian Antarctic Division, 2016c).

The earth is essentially a bar magnet with North and South Poles. But its magnetic field is shaped in the form of a comet due to the solar wind. In polar regions, this magnetic field is almost perpendicular to the surface of the earth facilitating the inflow of solar plasma (Schuch et al, 2001). And Polar Lights, Aurora Borealis and Aurora Australis, result when the sun's coronal ejections interfere with the earth's magnetic field (Lanzerotti and Weathermax, 2013, p. 214-215).

These Northern and Southern Lights occur in the upper atmosphere, typically 90 to 130 km above sea level. And this great height makes them visible at great distances. Polar Lights are present throughout the year. But they are only visible during the dark of winter (Hansen, 2016). And, although beautiful to the human eye, they interfere with human technology including electrical transmission and communication on land, at sea, in air, and in space (Lanzerotti and Weathermax, 2013, p. 214-215).

The most powerful solar storm ever recorded occurred in 1859 creating auroras around the world and disrupting telegraph systems in the United States and Europe (National Research Council, 2011, p. 6, 88). It was named the Carrington Event after the English astronomer Richard Carrington.

"Just before dawn the next day, skies all over planet Earth erupted in red, green, and purple auroras so brilliant that newspapers could be read as easily as in daylight" (National Aeronautics and Space Administration, 2016). One can imagine the disruption of a similar eruption today given the widespread dependence on modern electrical technology.

Another interesting visual phenomenon is known as looming. Atmospheric conditions in Antarctica sometimes permit observation below the horizon. And objects hundreds of kilometers away may appear much closer (Rubin, 2008, p. 36). This is due to the extreme refraction of light common in polar regions. Looming may be even more confusing than the mirror images of a desert mirage.

But it is nothing compared to a whiteout which results when light is reflected back and forth between an overcast sky and a surface of snow and/or ice. This phenomenon may result in a loss of both perspective and balance (Belanger, 2006, p. 75). Whiteouts are similar to blueouts over the Southern Ocean. Sometimes sky and sea appear to be the same color causing the horizon line to disappear.

Icebergs and islands then appear to float on a blue background (Rubin, 2008, p. 312).

Antarctic Exploration

The English expedition led by Edmond Halley in 1698 marked "the beginning of the exploration of the Southern Ocean and the Antarctic" and the one led by James Cook in 1768 "began to chart the real limits of the Southern Ocean for the first time" (Walton, 2013, p. 2).

The historical basis of French claims in Antarctica began in the 18th century with explorers such as de Lozier, du Fresne, de Tremarec, and d'Entrecasteaux and continued with d'Urville in the 19th century and Charcot in the 20th (Sulikowski, 2013, p. 167-168). But controversy continues to surround even the first sighting of the continent (Beck, 1986, p. 23) (Belanger, 2006, p. 8).

In 1819, the Russian expedition led by Fabian Gottlieb Thaddeus von Bellingshausen was the first to sight land within the Antarctic Circle, Peter I Island. And he was "the first to sight the Antarctic continent, if the edge of the … ice shelf … is considered as part of the continent" (Walton, 2013, p. 4-5).

On January 27, 1820, F.G.T. von Bellingshausen and Mikhail Lazarev of the Russian Imperial Navy were likely the first to sight the continent itself.

On January 30, 1820, Edward Bransfield and William Smith of the British Royal Navy were probably the second.

On November 18, 1820, Nathaniel Brown Palmer, an American sealer was likely the third (Connecticut Humanities, 2016).

On February 7, 1821, another America sealer, John Davis probably made the first landing in Antarctica (Orheim, 2013, p. 274). This was on the peninsula (as distinct from the continent).

In 1841, the Englishman James Clark Ross, sailing along the Ross Sea, claimed its eastern coast as Victoria Land (Berkman, 2002, p. 35).

In 1895, a Norwegian expedition led by Henryk Bull "was the first to first to land on the continent (as distinct from the peninsula) … the first to overwinter on land (Victoria Land), (and) the first to make a sledge journey on the Ross Ice Shelf" (Walton, 2013, p. 9-10).

In 1907-09, a British expedition led by Ernest Shackleton came within 97 miles of the South Pole. And the story of his heroic attempt to cross the continent in 1914-16 is legendary (Belanger, 2006, p. 11) (Rubin, 2008, p. 58-59) (Sitwell, 2009).

In 1911-12, the race to see who would be first to reach the South Pole garnered worldwide attention (Peterson, 1988, p. 33). This was the apex of the Heroic Age of Exploration (Klotz, 1990, p. 5). The Norwegian expedition under Roald Amundsen reached 90° S on December 14, 1911. The British expedition under Robert Scott reached the Pole on January 17, 1912, but all five of its members perished on their way back (Belanger, 2006, p. 11) (Rubin, 2008, p. 52-55).

The U.S. station at 90° S is named Amundsen-Scott in their honor. The Antarctic Explorer, a superb fold-up map, features a longer list of explorers, each with a picture and informational caption (Sitwell, 2009). The Heroic Age was not only about making discoveries and getting rich, it was also about "planting the flag" and "asserting territorial claims on behalf of the sovereign who sponsored these expeditions" (Rothwell, 2010, p. 17).

Territorial Claims

Seven nations have made sector claims to Antarctic territory. And two other nations have reserved the right to do so. These pie-shaped claims are drawn from the South Pole to arcs in the Southern Ocean (Belanger, 2006, p. 5, 16). A political map of the Antarctic Region is shown on the next page. It is provided by the U.S. Central Intelligence Agency (CIA) and shows both territorial claims and year-round research stations (University of Texas, 2016). The book, The Deep Freeze, by Dian Belanger provides excellent descriptions of U.S. research stations (2006). And the book, Science into Policy, by Paul Berkman is probably the best primary textbook on Antarctic research and government (2002).

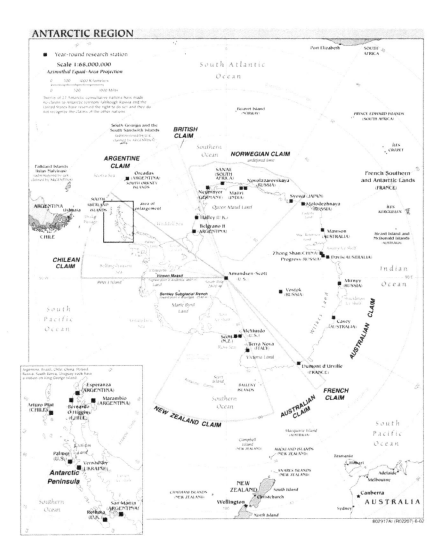

Before the Heroic Age of Exploration, the continent of Antarctica was terra incognita (unknown land) (Convey, Hughes, and Tin, 2012, p. 11). It was also res nullius (nobody's property) or terra nullius (nobody's land) due to the absence of indigenous people (Collis, 2010, p. 389) (Hemmings, 2012, p. 72, 75). Since then, seven countries have made specific claims to Antarctic territory. In this paper, the first five are fully counted, the sixth is partially counted, and the seventh is not counted at all for reasons given below:

In 1908, the United Kingdom, counterclockwise from 20° W to 80° W (80 – 20 = 60 degrees or 60 / 360 = 16.66% of Antarctica).

In 1923, New Zealand, counterclockwise from 150° W to 160° E (30 + 20 = 50 degrees or 50 / 360 = 13.89% of Antarctica).

In 1933, Australia, counterclockwise from 160° E to 45° E excluding the French sector (17 degrees 58 minutes + 91 degrees 11 minutes = 109 degrees 9 minutes or 6549 minutes / 21600 minutes = 30.32% of Antarctica). This represents the largest Antarctic claim. And the combined claims of the three Commonwealth nations comprise almost two thirds of Antarctic territory (Beck, 1986, p. 29).

In 1938, France, counterclockwise from 142°2′ E to 136°11′ E (5 degrees 51 minutes or 351 minutes / 21600 minutes = 1.63% of Antarctica). The initial claim of 1924 was imprecise (Joyner, 1998, p. 17). And the precise claim of 1938 fell within the Australian sector. But the three Commonwealth countries and France recognized each other's claims in 1938. And the "circle of mutual recognition expanded to include Norway the following year" (Klotz, 1990, p. 8, 12).

In 1939, Norway, counterclockwise from 45° E to 20° W but not quite a full sector to the South Pole (65 degrees or 65 / 360 = 18.06% of Antarctica). Norway eschewed the sector principle in the Antarctic to protect its claims in the Arctic (Beck, 1986, p. 126).

In 1940, Chile, counterclockwise from 53° W to 90° W but only 80° W to 90° W is counted (10 degrees or 10 / 360 = 2.77% of Antarctica) since the remainder overlaps the claims of both the United Kingdom and Argentina).

In 1946, Argentina, counterclockwise 25° W to 74°W is not counted since it overlaps the claims of both Britain and Chile. It should be noted that Argentina made "the first of several pronouncements

claiming title to Antarctic territory" in 1940 (Klotz, 1990, p. xxv).
And the controversy over these claims is commonly known as the
ABC dispute (Howard, 2013, p. 14).

The six counted claims leave an unclaimed portion, Marie Byrd
Land, counterclockwise from 90° W to 150° W (60 degrees or 60 /
360 = 16.66% of Antarctica).

It should be noted that both the United States and Russia "maintain a
claim on all of Antarctica based on their explorations" (Orheim,
2013, p. 276). Both have reserved the right to make an official claim
in the region (Beck, 1986, p. 124). And they have "asserted the
basis of claim alongside their repudiation of the seven overt claims"
listed above (Hemmings, 2012, p. 76).

In 1939, there was a secret Nazi expedition to Antarctica led by
Alfred Ritscher. 1.5 million darts inscribed with swastikas were
dropped from planes to establish sovereignty (Rubin, 2008, p. 64).
But German claims to the continent were never recognized despite
"expeditions in 1873, 1882-83, 1901-3, 1928-29, and 1939-40"
(Peterson, 1988, p. 64).

In 1946-47, the US Navy conducted Operation Highjump. It was officially a training exercise that brought 4700 men, 13 ships, and 33 aircraft to Antarctica and used both icebreakers and helicopters for the first time in the region (Rubin, 2008, p. 64).

In 1947, the Woman's International League for Peace and Freedom advocated that a UN committee take control of both the Arctic and the Antarctic. But this was impossible since the UN lacked any legal or other competence in polar regions (Triggs, 2011, p. 41).

In 1949, a tripartite agreement was signed by the ABC disputants (Argentina, Britain, and Chile) to limit "the deployment of warships south of 60 degrees S, and this agreement was renewed annually … until superseded by the Antarctic Treaty" in 1959 (Walton, 2013, p. 17).

In 1949, the "Soviet All-Union Geographic Society claimed that the Russian sailors Thaddeus Bellingshausen and Mikhail Lazarev had … been the first to discover parts of the Antarctic continent" (Klotz, 1990, p. 24).

In 1952, an Argentine shore party fired toward a British survey party at Hope Bay off the tip of the Antarctic Peninsula but no one was injured (Klotz, 1990, p. xxv).

In 1954, U.S. "President Eisenhower ... decided ... to continue the policy of asserting undefined 'rights' in the region" (ibid, p. 25). This was based in part on "Operation Highjump in 1946, which remains by far the largest expedition ever to take place in Antarctica" (Orheim, 2013, p. 277).

In 1955-56, the US Navy conducted Operation Deep Freeze I. This military operation effectively reopened Antarctica for scientific exploration just prior to the International Geophysical Year of 1957-58 (National Research Council, 2011, p. 75).

Regional Agreements

In the late 19th and early 20th centuries, scientific cooperation in the polar regions was "concentrated on the more accessible, more germane polar North" (Belanger, 2006, p. 2). But the first International Polar Year (IPY) from 1882 to 1883 featured some collaboration between the German expedition to the island of South

Georgia and the French expedition to the archipelago of Tierra del Fuego.

International cooperation on polar science was stopped in its tracks by World War I. And the second IPY from 1932 to 1933 focused almost exclusively on the Artic due to a lack of financing during the Great Depression (Summerhayes, 2013, p. 254). The Second World War had the same effect as the First. And due to the proximity of the Korean War from 1950 to 1953, the focus was once again on the Arctic (Belanger, 2006, p. 27).

The third IPY from 1957 to 1958 was renamed the International Geophysical Year (IGY). But "the main focus was again on the polar regions, and … the largest effort was in Antarctica" (Orheim, 2013, p. 280). This was "the turning point in Antarctic affairs … (as) twelve nations signed up to take part in the Antarctic component of the IGY" (Walton, 2013, p. 19-20): Argentina, Australia, Belgium, Chile, France, Japan, New Zealand, Norway, South Africa, the UK, the US, and USSR (now the Russian Federation). These nations subsequently met in the United States to discuss a regional agreement.

Antarctic Treaty

The Antarctic Treaty was signed by all twelve in Washington, DC, on December 1, 1959, and ratified by the twelfth on June 23, 1961 (Orheim, 2013, p. 281). The primary purpose of the Treaty, according to Article III (1), is to promote "international cooperation in scientific investigation." And "freedom of scientific investigation" is specifically protected under Article II of the Treaty.

According to Article VI, the Treaty applies to the area South of 60° S including ice shelves. It thus covers the entire continent and an area of the Southern Ocean beyond 66°33′ S, the Antarctic Circle (Rothwell, 2012a, p. 37).

Only seven nations have made formal claims to Antarctic territory: Argentina, Australia, Chile, France, New Zealand, Norway, and the UK although both Russia and the US have reserved the right to do so. It should be noted that Russian stations ring the continent and that one American base, Amundsen-Scott, is located where all claims intersect wedge-like at the South Pole (Beck, 1986, p. 72, 49)

The land and sea between 90° W and 150° W (60 of 360 degrees or 16.66%) remains officially unclaimed by any nation. But the unclaimed status of this area has not prevented it from being considered part of the area covered by the Antarctic Treaty at least insofar as the parties to the Treaty are concerned (Beck, 1986, p. 135).

Article IV of the Treaty is designed to "preserve the status quo … (and) "no new claims have been made to Antarctica by any state" (Rothwell, 2012a, p. 35, 38, 45). The Treaty formally codifies a gentlemen's agreement, modus vivendi, (Klotz, 1990, p. 47) to disagree on the matter of sovereignty (Vidas, 1996a, p. 37).

In addition to the three categories of non-claimants, claimants, and semi-claimants (the US and Russia), there are six categories of Treaty membership based on Article IX. They are broken down into three sets: first, non-parties and parties; second, non-Consultative Parties and Consultative Parties; and, third, conditional Consultative Parties and unconditional Consultative Parties.

The unconditional category represents the original twelve contracting parties to the Treaty (Article IX (1). The conditional category represents those nations that subsequently acceded to the Treaty and continued to demonstrate an interest in Antarctica by conducting research there (Article IX (2). Both unconditional and conditional Consultative Parties are entitled to appoint representatives to participate in Consultative Meetings.

According to Article XII (1), the Treaty may be "modified or amended at any time by unanimous agreement" of those entitled to participate in Consultative Meetings. Although non-Consultative Parties have been permitted to attend these meetings since 1983, they lack any formal decision-making power (Vidas, 1996a, p. 55).

The first Antarctic Treaty Consultative Meeting was held in 1961 (Klotz, 1990, p. xxvi). ATCMs were biennial until 1994 and annual thereafter. They are hosted by Consultative Parties in alphabetical order using the English spelling of country names (Secretariat of the Antarctic Treaty, 2016f).

The Treaty "contributes to demilitarizing and denuclearizing one tenth of the earth's surface" (Joyner, 2013, p. 113). Article I (1) stipulates that "Antarctica shall be used for peaceful purposes only." And Article V (1) stipulates that "nuclear explosions ... and the disposal … of radioactive waste … shall be prohibited." Antarctica is in fact "the world's oldest nuclear-weapons-free zone" (Peterson, 1988, p. 222).

Article VII gives designated observers "complete freedom of access … to all areas of Antarctica" mandating that "all stations … be open at all times to inspection." It also permits "aerial observation … over … all areas of Antarctica" by designated observers. But enforcement of Treaty provisions is problematic since its administrative body, the Secretariat, has no power beyond what is necessary to carry out its own functions (Jabour, 2010, p. 28).

Article I (2) makes clear that military activities in support of "scientific research or … any other peaceful purpose" is permissible. But there is no provision for an Antarctic police force and there are no such forces stationed anywhere on the continent. And "the effect of Article VIII (1) is to reaffirm jurisdiction based on nationality" (Rothwell, 2012b, p. 138, 137).

The soldiers and sailors of contracting parties are capable of acting as peace officers on land and at sea. And the significance of the military for law enforcement purposes is that they "possess a

capability to engage in law enforcement activities, especially at sea"
(Rothwell, 2012b, p.151, 138). But "law enforcement in Antarctica
has always been problematic because of uncertainty regarding
sovereignty and jurisdiction" (Davis, 2007, p. 143).

A copy of the original Antarctic Treaty is found at the website of the
Secretariat (2016a):

http://www.ats.aq/documents/ats/treaty_original.pdf

There are currently 29 Consultative Parties and 24 non-Consultative
Parties to the Treaty. An up-to-date list of the 53 parties to the
Antarctic Treaty is also found at the website of the Secretariat
(2016d): http://www.ats.aq/devas/ats_parties.aspx?lang=e

ATS

The Antarctic Treaty System (ATS) operates according to the 1959
Antarctic Treaty including the 1964 Agreed Measures for the
Conservation of Antarctic Fauna and Flora (AMCAFF), the 1972
Convention for the Conservation of Antarctic Seals (CCAS), the
1980 Convention on the Conservation of Antarctic Marine Living
Resources (CCAMLR), and the 1991 (Madrid) Protocol on

Environmental Protection to the Antarctic Treaty (Rothwell, Scott, and Hemmings, 2012, 1). But "the ATS has limited grip on actors that are not subjected to the jurisdiction of Contracting Parties to the relevant ATS-instruments (third-state activities)" (Bastmeijer, 2011, p. 28).

AMCAFF

The Agreed Measures for the Conservation of Antarctic Fauna and Flora was signed in 1964 by the Consultative Parties and entered into force in 1964 (Berkman, 2009, p. 531). It applies to the area of the Antarctic Treaty, south of 60° S, including all ice shelves. The Treaty itself "is silent on the questions of whether to permit and how to regulate the exploitation of Antarctic and Southern Ocean resources" (Peterson, 1988, p. 49).

The AMCAFF protects native mammals, native birds, and native plants. But biodiversity is extremely low on the continent. Most life exists in the sea. Algal blooms in the summer provide food for invertebrates such as krill. And these provide food for fish and "higher predators including penguins, whales, seals, and flying birds" (Hughes and Convey, 2014, p. 1-2). A list of the Agreed

Measures can be found at the Center for International Earth Science Information Network (2016):

http://sedac.ciesin.org/entri/texts/acrc/aff64.txt.html

CCAS

The Convention for the Conservation of Antarctic Seals was signed in 1972 and entered into force in 1978 (Orheim, 2013, p. 296). The CCAS specifically protects seals. And whales are specifically protected outside the ATS by the International Whaling Commission. The CCAS is found at the website of the Secretariat of Antarctic Treaty (2016c):

http://www.ats.aq/documents/recatt/Att076_e.pdf

CCAMLR

The Convention on the Conservation of Antarctic Marine Living Resources was signed in 1980 and entered into force in 1982 (Orheim, 2013, p. 296). CCAMLR (pronounced camel-R) first as a Convention and later as a Commission "has provided leadership in a number of key areas" including: application of the precautionary principle and the ecosystems approach; and, curtailment of illegal, unreported, and unregulated (IUU) fishing and the incidental catch of seabirds in longline fisheries (Haward, 2012, p. 222, 235).

24 states plus the European Union are members of the current Commission. And 23 of the 24 states are Consultative Parties to the Antarctic Treaty. The 24th, Namibia, is neither a Consultative Party nor a non-Consultative Party to the Treaty (Commission for the Conservation of Antarctic Marine Living Resources, 2016b). Nine other states, although they are not members, have acceded to the Convention (Commission for the Conservation of Antarctic Marine Living Resources, 2016a).

CCAMLR applies in Southern Ocean beyond 60° S, the Antarctic Treaty boundary, to the Antarctic Convergence. Since the Convergence fluctuates (as described later), the Convention publishes specific geographic coordinates (Klotz, 1990, p. 74) between 60° S and 50° S to define its outer limits (Redgwell, p. 210).

The area of jurisdiction is then broken down into subareas and divisions using a Conservation Grid (Joyner, 1998, p. 135). And the rules of CCAMLR are transparent as well as non-discriminatory so they satisfy the key requirements of World Trade Organization (WTO) (Haward, 2012, p. 232). The Convention is found at the website of the Secretariat of the Antarctic Treaty (2016b):

http://www.ats.aq/documents/ats/ccamlr_e.pdf

CRAMRA (not ratified)

Whereas CCAMLR deals with life in the surrounding sea, the 1988 Convention on the Regulation of Antarctic Mineral Resource Activities (CRAMRA) would have dealt with drilling and mining had it been ratified. It featured a strict regulatory regime to protect the environment. But due to pressure from 3rd World nations and green groups, both Australia and France "refused to participate" (Joyner, 2013, p. 119). Instead Australia and France supported the Protocol on Environmental Protection.

PEPAT (Madrid Protocol)

The Protocol on Environmental Protection to the Antarctic Treaty, more commonly known as the Environmental or Madrid Protocol, was signed in 1991 and entered into force in 1998 (Orheim, 2013, p. 289) after it was ratified by the Consultative Parties that originally

signed the Protocol in 1991 (Australian Antarctic Division, 2016b).
Its advisory body, the Committee for Environmental Protection
(CEP), was organized in 1998 (Dudeney and Walton, 2012, p. 2).

The Protocol placed an indefinite ban on the exploitation of non-
living resources (Sulikowski, 2013, p. 174) and thus rendered moot
the Question of Antarctica that was placed before the United Nations
General Assembly in 1983 (Hemmings, 2014, p. 3). And, in 2005,
the Question was finally removed from the active agenda of the
UNGA (Hamzah, 2013, p. 96-99).

The Protocol was clearly a victory for green groups advocating a
World Park and the conservation of resources (Bastmeijer, 2011, p.
23-24). But it was ironically a defeat for 3rd World nations
promoting the Common Heritage of Mankind (CHM) and a
redistribution of wealth. It was also a defeat for nations favoring
CRAMRA which offered a balance between economic development
and environmental protection.

The Protocol applies to all activities in the Antarctic Treaty area
(Joyner, 1998, p. 81). But "the protection of … geological … values
has not featured as prominently as the protection of biological

values" (Hughes et al, 2016, p. 5). Like CAMMLR, the Protocol applies beyond 60° S to the Antarctic Convergence in an area of the Southern Ocean described as "the Antarctic Marine ecosystem" (Berkman, 2002, p. 176-177).

The Protocol is described as a "comprehensive regime for the protection of the Antarctic environment and dependent and associated ecosystems" (Secretariat of the Antarctic Treaty, 2016e). It is found at the website of Secretariat of the Antarctic Treaty (2016e): http://www.ats.aq/documents/recatt/Att006_e.pdf

SCAR

The Special (later Scientific) Committee on Antarctic Research was established 1958, the year before the Antarctic Treaty was signed. Its members initially defined Antarctica as bounded by the Antarctic Convergence but, in 2005, they defined a larger area as bounded by the sub-Antarctic Front, the northern boundary of the Antarctic Circumpolar Current (Scientific Committee on Antarctic Research, 2016b).

The Committee became the informal but effective scientific mechanism for the Antarctic Treaty Consultative Parties and was instrumental in the development of the 1964 Agreed Measures. SCAR became an observer under CCAMLR at the first meeting of the Commission in 1982. Its influence in the ATS declined due to its partisan opposition to CRAMRA in 1988. But, after 1998, SCAR's influence rebounded as a permanent observer in CEP (Hemmings, 2010, p. 7).

SCAR is an inter-disciplinary committee of the International Council for Science (still known as the ICSU after its former name, the International Council of Scientific Unions (Scientific Committee on Antarctic Research, 2016a). Its membership consists of 37 nations and 9 ICSU Scientific Unions. To achieve full voting status, a member must demonstrate an interest in Antarctic science with an active research program (Lopez-Martinez and Sparrow, 2014, p. 128).

ATS v the World

The Antarctic Treaty System is not a homogenous organization. It is bifocal in that it "allows claimant and non-claimants to pursue their respective interest through the system" (Howard, 2013, p. 18). It is trifocal if one adds a category of semi-claimants for the US and Russia, countries that have reserved the right to make claims in the future; and, it is quadrifocal if one adds a category of counter-claimants for Argentina, Britain, and Chile (the ABC countries with overlapping claims) (Dodds, 2012, p. 108, 114).

The ATS is nonetheless viewed by the 3rd World as an exclusive club that monopolizes Antarctic resources (Beck, 1986, p. 289). Developing nations complain that the region is "controlled by a select group … making international law and Antarctic policy explicitly for themselves and implicitly for the international community" (Joyner, 1998, 48). Yet these same developing nations are not at all shy about exercising their own sovereign rights and monopolizing their own natural resources

Although the 3rd World could be viewed by the ATS as an unruly mob, the club has attempted to deal with the Antarctic Problem by recognizing all interested nations one way or another. For example, the number of Consultative Parties to the Antarctic Treaty has grown from 12 in 1950 to 29 today.

In addition, there are now 24 non-Consultative Parties that "are invited to attend the Consultative Meetings but do not participate in the decision-making" (Secretariat the Antarctic Treaty, 2016d). But, in general, attempts by the ATS to please everyone have in fact pleased no one particularly those in 3rd World.

India put the Question of Antarctica on the agenda of the United Nations General Assembly in 1956. But its support for the internationalization of the continent in the form of a UN trusteeship was dropped after objections from Chile and Argentina (Elzinga, 2013, p. 200).

"The United Nations ... debates on the Question of Antarctica ... ensued from Malaysia's (anti-colonial) critique ... cleverly sold to like-minded countries from the South ... (using) the popular concept of the Common Heritage of Mankind (advocated by Malta)" (Hamzah, 2013, p. 96-97).

In 1983, the Question of Antarctica was formally addressed by the UN for the first time. But the debate "as well as discussions in subsequent years failed to bridge the gap between critics and supporters" (Klotz, 1990, p. 110-111).

Public opinion and policy among the Consultative Parties is gradually shifting from idealism to realism. For example, "New Zealand's initiative in helping Malaysia to take a positive role in Antarctica illustrates how … it manages to both uphold the Antarctic Treaty and to maintain its own claimant rights" (Brady, 2013, p. 159).

But after "proposing that Antarctica should be managed by the United Nations or run as a world park … (there was) a gradual realization that collective action … would not always … protect New Zealand's national interests" (ibid, p. 149).

International Law

IWC

In 1946, International Convention on the Regulation of Whaling was established followed by the International Whaling Commission (Whale and Dolphin Conservation, 2016). Its 1980 moratorium on all commercial catches became effective in 1986. And, in 1994, the IWC established the Southern Ocean Whale Sanctuary (Rubin, 2008, p. 101).

But the sanctuary is ineffective due to "the IWC's failure so far to organize long-term surveillance of the region" (Antarctic and Southern Ocean Coalition, 2016c). "Some states prioritize conservation, while others favor sustainable exploitation" and some states such as Japan ignore the ICRW altogether "under the guise of scientific research" (Plant, 2015, p. 40).

IMO

The 1948, the Inter-governmental Maritime Consultative Organization was established. It became operationally effective in 1959. In 1982, its name was changed to the International Maritime Organization. The IMO is specialized agency of the UN whose mission is "is to promote safe, secure, environmentally sound, efficient and sustainable shipping through cooperation" (International Maritime Organization, 2016a). But inspection and monitoring are responsibilities of numerous states making uniform enforcement problematic (Craig, 2010, p. 16)

UNCLOS

UNCLOS was signed in 1982 replacing the UN maritime treaties of 1958. The United Nations Convention on the Law of the Sea (United Nations, 2016b) can be found in its entirety at:

http://www.un.org/depts/los/convention_agreements/texts/unclos/un clos_e.pdf

UNCLOS became effective in 1994. But implementation was left to other organizations including the International Whaling Commission (IWC), the International Maritime Organization (IMO), and International Seabed Authority (ISA) (discussed later). Enforcement was left to member nations. And such delegation of authority to other organizations and member nations makes the implementation and enforcement of maritime law problematic.

Territorial Sea (12 NM)

According to Article 2: "The sovereignty of a coastal State extends, beyond its land territory and internal waters and, in the case of an archipelagic State, its archipelagic waters, to an adjacent belt of sea, described as the territorial sea. This sovereignty extends to the air space over the territorial sea as well as to its bed and subsoil."

According to Article 3: "Every State has the right to establish the breadth of its territorial sea up to a limit not exceeding 12 nautical miles (13.8 statute miles or 22.2 kilometers), measured from baselines determined in accordance with this Convention."

According to Article 5: "Except where otherwise provided in this Convention, the normal baseline for measuring the breadth of the territorial sea is the low-water line along the coast as marked on large-scale charts officially recognized by the coastal State."

Contiguous Zone (24 NM)

According to Article 33 (1): "In a zone contiguous to its territorial sea, described as the contiguous zone, the coastal State may exercise the control necessary to: (a) prevent infringement of its customs, fiscal, immigration or sanitary laws and regulations within its territory or territorial sea; (b) punish infringement of the above laws and regulations committed within its territory or territorial sea."

According to Article 33 (2): "The contiguous zone may not extend beyond 24 nautical miles (27.6 statute miles or 44.4 kilometers) from the baselines from which the breadth of the territorial sea is measured."

Exclusive Economic Zone (200 NM)

According to Article 56: "In the exclusive economic zone, the coastal State has: sovereign rights for the purpose of exploring and exploiting, conserving and managing the natural resources, whether living or non-living, of the waters superjacent to the seabed and of the seabed and its subsoil, and with regard to other activities for the economic exploitation and exploration of the zone, such as the production of energy from the water, currents and winds."

According to Article 57: "The exclusive economic zone shall not extend beyond 200 nautical miles (230 statute miles or 370 kilometers) from the baselines from which the breadth of the territorial sea is measured."

Continental Shelves and Extended Continental Shelves

Baselines defined as low water lines are confusing in Antarctica due to coastal ice. Otherwise, the Law of the Sea is fairly straightforward with regard to Territorial Seas, Contiguous Zones, and Exclusive Economic Zones. The LOS is however extremely confusing with regard to Continental Shelves and Extended Continental Shelves (Craig, 2016, p. 15-17). Ambiguous wording with regard to the seabed adjacent the continents makes interpretation and enforcement of international law difficult if not impossible. And confusion not only exists with respect to the delimitation of claims but also with respect to the distribution of wealth through the International Seabed Authority.

ISA

The International Seabed Authority is an autonomous international organization. But it was established under UNCLOS (International Seabed Authority, 2016a).

According to Article 82: "The coastal State shall make payments or contributions in kind in respect to the exploitation of the non-living resources of the continental shelf beyond 200 nautical miles …

annually … after the first five years … for the sixth year, the rate …

shall be 1 percent of the value or volume of production … (and)

increase by 1 percent for each subsequent year until the twelfth year

and shall remain at 7 per cent thereafter … through the Authority,

which shall distribute them to States Parties to this Convention."

International Agreements

The 1993 Agreement to Promote Compliance with International

Conservation and Management Measures by Fishing Vessels on the

High Seas (the Compliance Agreement) applies to large parts of the

Southern Ocean. But it relies on "Flag State Responsibility" (United

Nations, 2016c). And reliance on flag-state jurisdiction means it is

difficult if not impossible to control the activities of ships flying the

flags of nations that are not parties to the various Conventions

(Peterson, 1988, p. 110).

The 1995 United Nations Fish Stocks Agreement (UNFSA)

"reinforces the roles of regional fisheries management organizations

(RFMOs) … (with) significant non-flag state enforcement powers"

(Haward, 2012, p. 220-221). It applies to Straddling Fish Stocks and

Highly Migratory Fish Stocks including those in the Southern Ocean, both in "areas under national jurisdiction and the adjacent high seas" (United Nations, 2016a). But it is difficult to ensure that measures taken are uniformly enforced.

The 2009 Food and Agriculture Organization (FAO) Agreement on Port State Measures to Prevent, Deter and Eliminate Illegal, Unreported and Unregulated (IUU) Fishing went into effect in 2016. It is designed to prevent "ill-caught fish from being offloaded and sold" and to share information on "unscrupulous vessels" (United Nations, 2016d). But only 25 nations are currently members including four claimants to Antarctic territory (Australia, Chile, New Zealand, and Norway) and one semi-claimant (the United States).

Unsettled Disputes and Pending Claims

The International Whaling Commission "declared a moratorium on commercial whaling in 1980, and established a whale sanctuary in the Southern Ocean in 1994" (Mossop, 2012, p. 308). But the dispute between Japan and Australia over whaling goes well beyond the dispute between Japan and the IWC. "Japan considers the Southern Ocean to be the high seas, and Australia's claim to jurisdiction rests on an exclusive economic zone declared off its ATT (Australian Antarctic Territory)" (Mossop, 2012, p. 316).

Article IV (2) of the Antarctic Treaty stipulates that "no new claim, or enlargement of an existing claim, to territorial sovereignty in Antarctica shall be asserted while the present Treaty is in force." But Article 76 of the U.N. Convention on the Law of the Sea stipulates that "the coastal State exercises over the continental shelf sovereign rights for the purpose of exploring it and exploiting its natural resources." Such confusion leads some to question "the ability of any state to regard itself as a coastal state" in Antarctica (Davis, 2007, p. 151).

All seven Antarctic claimants are parties to UNCLOS and "assert that they are coastal states" (Hemmings and Stephens, 2010, p. 313). And, in spite of and/or because of legal ambiguity, all seven claimant nations have submitted full or partial claims to the UN Commission on the Limits of the Continental Shelf (CLCS): Australia in 2004, New Zealand in 2006, Argentina in 2009, Norway in 2009, Chile in 2009, the UK in 2009, and France with two claims in 2009 (United Nations, 2016f).

It should be noted that Chile made its submission only in the form of a Preliminary Information statement (Joyner, 2013, p. 115). It should also be noted that "the CLCS does not have the competence to adjudicate between competing coastal states" including the ABC dispute between Argentina, Britain, and Chile (Dodds, 2011, p. 237).

And it should be noted that the Extended Continental Shelves of sub-Antarctic islands extending into the Antarctic Treaty area have "attracted no substantive attention" as yet even though "the sovereignty of states over these islands is generally accepted" (Hemmings and Stephens, 2010, p. 314, 319).

If a claimant attempts to enforce a 200-mile Exclusive Economic Zone south of 60° S, "the fundamental compromise on which the entire Antarctic Treaty is constructed would be undermined" (Klotz, 1990, p. 86). But, given the interest that many nations have expressed with regard to Antarctic resources, it is only prudent for claimants to reassert their sovereign rights.

And it is probably time for the United States and Russia to make specific claims in the unclaimed portion of Antarctica and to recognize the existing claims of the United Kingdom, New Zealand,

Australia, France, and Norway. It is also probably time for Chile and Argentina to resolve their overlapping claims with each other and with Britain.

In 1952, the Argentines fired warning shots at the British near the tip of the Antarctic Peninsula. In 1982, they lost a major war to the Brits over the Falkland Islands. And, in 2012, tensions between the two rose again after a major oil find near the Falkland Islands. It should be noted that "Antarctica is estimated to have the third largest oil reserves after Saudi Arabia and Venezuela (Basken, 2012, p. 2-3).

Science and Business

The first International Polar Year (IPY) in 1882-83 featured two island observation stations near Antarctica: a German one on South Georgia and a French one in Tierra del Fuego. The second IPY in 1932-33 focused mainly on the Arctic due to the shortage of funds available for research during the global economic depression.

The third IPY, in 1957-58, renamed the International Geographical Year (IGY), brought scientists from 67 countries to Antarctica.

Although it was essentially a civilian exercise, it depended upon military support for logistics. The fourth IGY in 2007-09 strengthened not only international collaboration but also interdisciplinary approaches particularly with respect to global warming (Summerhayes, 2013, p. 254, 253, 267-269).

There are now 40 permanent research stations in Antarctica, 30 summer only stations, and numerous field camps. An interactive map of main facilities is provided by the Council of Managers of National Antarctic Programs (COMNAP, 2016ba):

https://ucnz.maps.arcgis.com/apps/webappviewer/index.html?id=86 63617ffa264e45aa3804d0d08fcdf8

In the winter, it is almost impossible to deliver supplies anywhere on the continent. And, even in the summer, bad weather can interrupt deliveries by ship or plane. Freshwater is a precious commodity. So, on the coast, seawater is desalinated (through osmosis) and, farther inland, snow and ice are melted.

Research installations generally rely on diesel fuel for their generators. But it too must be transported at least initially via sea or air. Snowmobiles and polar tractors are plagued not only by cold weather but also by mountainous terrain, deep crevasses, and thin ice. And, during midwinter, visibility is a problem since it is dark 24 hours a day (Sanson, 2013, p. 229, 236, 237, 239, 250).

The extremes of winter dark and summer light can cause both physical and mental health problems similar to jet lag and shift work. Living in isolation can lower immunity to disease and increase susceptibility to depression. Working in small groups for long periods presents challenges involving the interactions of different personality types (Rubin, 2008, p. 162-163, 330). The physical dangers of frostbite and hypothermia are of course ever present. And operations on sea are as dangerous as those on land.

Sea ice is frozen ocean water. It is a seasonal phenomenon that reaches its winter-maximum in September and October. Along the western coast of the Antarctic Peninsula, sea ice peaks in a regular cycle every five to seven years. And icebergs calved from continental glaciers, ice sheets, and ice shelves are hazardous to shipping around the entire continent.

The Southern Ocean is also feared for its extreme weather especially cyclonic storms (rotating clockwise in the Southern Hemisphere).

"Strong westerly winds … circle the … continent (clockwise) … (and) the longest current in the world … the Antarctic Circumpolar Current (also known as the West Wind Drift) … moves eastward around the continent (clockwise)" (National Research Council, 2011, p. 3, 19).

The average flow of the Antarctic Circumpolar Current (ACC) is four times greater than the Gulf Stream (Rubin, 2008, p. 147). And storms in the Southern Ocean produce not only "the strongest westerly winds on the planet … (but also) extremely large wave heights" (National Research Council, 2011, p. 35, 45). The marine area from the Antarctic coast to the Polar Front, where polar air meets tropical air, is roughly 35 million square km (Jabour, 2012, p. 238-239).

This roughly coincides with the area covered by CAMMLR and the Madrid Protocol bounded by the Antarctic Convergence where colder and saltier Antarctic water meets warmer and fresher sub-Antarctic water. The Convergence is a natural boundary forming a biological barrier that limits the migration of most species (Joyner,

1998, p. 116). It effectively separates the Southern Ocean from the three major oceans of the world: Atlantic, Indian, and Pacific.

The Antarctic Convergence varies not only in its width but also in its distance from the continent according to the seasons and the currents. It fluctuates between 20 and 30 miles wide and averages about 1000 miles offshore. The Convergence is north of the northern limit of sea ice except for one small area beyond the tip of the Antarctic Peninsula. It is also north of 60° S, the Antarctic Treaty boundary, as well as 66°33' S, the Arctic Circle (Klotz, 1990, p. 40-43.

In the subsections that follow, various categories of science and business in Antarctica are listed and discussed alphabetically:

Astronomy

"Antarctica is a rich source for meteorites, providing astrobiologists with clues to the origin of life in the universe" (Lanzerotti and Weathermax, 2013, p. 223). "Antarctica has a number of important advantages for studies of space related phenomena" including its large land mass, high elevation, and radio quiet areas due to a limited human presence (Lanzerotti and Weathermax, 2013, p. 217-218, 220).

Space weather is best monitored from the polar regions since interference from the alignment of the earth's magnetic field is less problematic at higher latitudes. Refer to the illustration of magnetic field lines provided by Crystalinks:

http://www.crystalinks.com/earthsmagneticfield.html

Furthermore, astronomical objects viewed from either pole never rise nor set. Their elevation in the sky is constant permitting long and uniform observation. But land based stations at the South Pole are far more stable than sea based stations at the North Pole (National Research Council, 2011, p. 7, 94).

At both poles, the atmosphere is flattened by the rotation of the earth. And water vapor is squeezed out by the extreme cold. This results in thin and dry air that is perfect for studying celestial objects and phenomena (Rubin, 2008, p. 332). "Antarctica is an ideal location to conduct … astronomical observations" given not only its location on land but also its cold dry air and stable atmospheric conditions (Lanzerotti and Weathermax, 2013, p. 222).

Bioprospecting

"Bioprospecting does not attract special legal attention in the Antarctic" inasmuch as "sample collection is scientific research ... with no major environmental implications" (Jabour, 2013, p. 242, 250). There is however considerable overlap between science and business, pure science and applied science, and research and development (Beck, 1986, p. 102). "Much Antarctic science plays an indirect or, even occasionally, a direct role in facilitating resource development ... (and) competition over resources constitutes a ... threat, to the security of the continent and the wider region" (Scott, 2012, p. 293).

Bioprospecting does attract special legal attention from rent-seekers in the 3rd World who demand a share of any profitable endeavor based on the Common Heritage of Mankind. But "exclusive reward from bioprospecting is as legitimate as exclusive reward from fishing ... (and) describing taxa in the academic literature, will suffice in terms of obligations to all mankind" as set forth in the Antarctic Treaty (Jabour, 2010, p. 28) (Jabour, 2013, p. 254-255).

Likewise, a central principle in patent law requires applicants to describe their inventions openly and completely in writing. The Agreement on Trade-Related Aspects of Intellectual Property Rights (TRIPS) requires that member nations guarantee the owner "an exclusive right which excludes third parties from 'making, using, offering for sale, selling, or importing' that product" or process for a period of twenty years (Guyomard, 2010, p. 35).

Likewise, "the Convention on Biological Diversity is firmly based on the principle of national territoriality" (Guyomard, 2010, p. 34). According to the CBD, "states have the lawful right to use genetic material in … their territory as they deem appropriate" (Joyner, 2012, p. 206-207). The number of patents involving biological material in Antarctica is rapidly increasing. And developing countries insist on sharing the benefits (but not the costs) (Tvedt, 2009, p. 1-6).

The most daunting legal problems in Antarctica involve piracy of intellectual property on the one hand and expropriation of company profit on the other as the 3rd World attempts to pick both pockets by advocating the Common Heritage of Mankind. And "the practice of supporting 'non-nationals' though national programs will … lead to complications in determining subsequent ownership of IPR" (intellectual property rights) (Hughes and Bridge, 2010, p. 16).

Fishing

"Fish, if managed correctly, are a renewable resource … (whereas) hydrocarbons and minerals are, so far as is known today, nonrenewable" (Peterson, 1988, p. 158). But illegal, unregulated, and unreported fishing (IUU) is a growing problem in the Southern Ocean since fish stocks elsewhere are collapsing (Dodds, 2010, p. 112). There is particular concern about "the rise of the Chinese fishing fleet as it increasingly enters the Southern Ocean" (Joyner, 2013, p. 121). And, in so vast region, it is difficult to prevent not only IUU fishing but also shipping accidents that result in pollution of the environment.

Mining and Drilling

Lake Whillans is 640 km from the South Pole near the Ross Sea. It is a subsurface lake trapped beneath 800 m of ice. The lake is 60 square km in area but only 2 m deep. Researchers drilling into the lake have been careful to avoid any contamination that might introduce invasive organisms. They have already found a density of microbial life similar to the benthos of the world's deep oceans, almost 4,000 species of bacteria and archaea, showing that life has survived there without energy from the sun for at least 120,000 years (Fox, 2014).

Climate change occurred in Antarctica more than 200 million years ago. And it became warm enough and wet enough for the growth of temperate forests and swamps (Storey, 2013, p. 48). The decay of plant matter eventually formed the deposits of today's fossil fuels including coal, oil, and gas. One extensive coal seam is located in the Transantarctic Mountains between East and West Antarctica (Berkman, 2002, p. 56, 83, 190). But mining for coal is difficult, as is mining for anything else on land, due to the extreme cold. And drilling for oil and gas or anything else is even more problematic due to all the ice.

The situation offshore is however far worse. Drilling in the Southern Ocean is fraught with difficulty and danger. The continental shelf is the deepest in the world, the ocean is covered with ice most of the year, and wellheads are vulnerable to icebergs scouring the seabed. Cleanup operations from well blowouts and tanker spills at the end of summer could be delayed for a year. And cold water would retard the process of natural degradation year 'round (Klotz, 1990, p. 90, 95).

Offshore resources include not only oil and gas but also manganese nodules on the seabed. And it is possible that icebergs will considered a mineral resource if they can be towed to adjacent lands where water is in short supply. Onshore resources include not only coal but also chromium, cobalt, copper, gold, graphite, iron, lead, molybdenum, nickel, silver, titanium, uranium, and zinc (Beck, 1986, p. 239, 261-262).

Rare earth minerals may be the first to be exploited since prices are high enough to offset the extremely high cost of Antarctic operations (Rodger, 2013, p. 323). But any commercial activity is "unrealistic at present levels of technology" (Orheim, 2013, p. 286) and "it is currently not financially viable to extract … mineral resources from Antarctica" (Storey, 2013, p. 66).

The situation is however likely to change as supplies elsewhere are exploited to exhaustion and as overall consumer demand increases with the exploding population of the world. Resource extraction in Antarctica is also likely to become more attractive if 3rd World nations, particularly African and Muslim nations, become even less stable and even more violent. Political risk is an important factor in any decision to invest.

Tourism

The commercial stages of Antarctic history run from sealing, whaling, and fishing to tourism (Basberg, 2010, p. 228) (Bastmeijer, 2011, p. 16-17). Tourism is now the most important commercial development in Antarctica (Dodds, 2010, p. p. 113). It was not mentioned in the Antarctic Treaty inasmuch as it was not a "foreseeable phenomenon" (Verbitsky, 2013, p. 222). But, with stronger ships and warmer weather, the number of Antarctic tourists has increased over the years (Bastmeijer, 2001, p. 24, 34). And their environmental impact has increased as well.

This includes the interruption of breeding cycles from noise and light pollution as well as mere human presence. It also includes the introduction of alien species including "seeds and other organisms inadvertently tagged to their shoes or clothes ... with climate change rendering Antarctica increasingly hospitable to species from temperate climes" (Economist, 2012).

In addition to possible contamination onshore from visitors, there is possible pollution offshore from passenger ships. The ban by the International Maritime Organization on the carriage and use of heavy fuel oil on vessels in Antarctic waters (effective in 2011) has resulted in fewer large and mid-size vessels in the region (Convey, Hughes, and Tin, 2012, p. 4-5). But there is considerable inconsistency since "the enforcement of IMO conventions depends upon the Governments of Member Parties" (International Maritime Organization, 2016b).

The International Association of Antarctic Tour Operators was founded in 1991 as an industry group that promotes "safe and environmentally sound private-sector travel" (International Association of Antarctic Tour Operators, 2016). The IAATO "has been proactive in implementing biosecurity practices for tourists and staff going ashore" (Hughes and Pertierra, 2016, p. 152). And the

IAATO works closely with the Antarctic Treaty System. But it "does not have any regulatory authority" and many non-IAATO passenger ships have entered into ATS waters (Dodds, 2010, p. 113).

Climate Change

Human activity, whether scientific or commercial, is facilitated by a warming climate. And the range of most species, including plants as well as animals, is projected to shift toward the poles. Although most of Antarctica has experienced very little warming, the temperature has been rising on the western side of the continent for the past 50 years (Turner et al, 2014, p. 3).

At the Palmer Station, on the northwest coast of the Antarctic Peninsula, the average winter air temperature has increased by 6°C since 1950 (National Research Council, 2011, p. 61, 64). And the number of gentoo penguins has increased at 32 of 45 sites along the Peninsula due to a more hospitable climate (Turner et al, p. 4).

The West Antarctic Ice Sheet is grounded below sea level. Its floating ice shelves are also exposed to the warming of subsurface ocean currents resulting in basal melt. A total disintegration of the

WAIS would result in a global sea level rise of about 3.3 m (Diaz and Keller, 2016, p. 608). This is one of many potential catastrophes that constitute the bread and butter of green groups.

But it is a "sore spot among WAIS scientists" as to whether the ice sheet will grow due to additional snowfall or shrink due to additional melting of the sheet and calving of icebergs (O'Reilly, Oreskes, and Oppenheimer, 2012, p. 710). Some are predicting that future warming will lead to increasing snowfall and a larger ice sheet (Thomas, 2014, p. 307).

Although "the Earth system has been cooling ... superimposed on this long-term cooling trend are short term climate fluctuations" (Berkman, 2002, p. 95). "The anthropogenic climate change signal during the second half of the twentieth century is small compared to the noise associated with natural climate variability" (Previdi and Polvani, 2016, p. 1). The climate is always changing and it is influenced by many factors including: the albedo feedback; greenhouse gases; the earth's orbit, wobble, and tilt; the ozone layer; solar activity; and, volcanic eruptions.

Albedo Feedback

The ice-albedo feedback effect is produced as less sunlight is reflected from water and land than from clouds, snow, and ice (Ohio State University, 2008). Albedo is Latin for whiteness and whiteness is a measure of reflectivity. It is a ratio ranging from one, or perfectly white, to zero, or perfectly black. And a decrease in sea ice and snow due to warming will result in additional warming due to reduced reflectivity or albedo (a smaller ratio of light reflected to light received). "Ice and snow reflect some 85 percent of solar radiation … (whereas) open water … absorbs 93 percent" (Isaacson, 2016, p. 107).

Greenhouse Gasses

Greenhouse gases, including water vapor and carbon dioxide, absorb infrared radiation reflected from the surface of the Earth trapping heat in the troposphere (the lowest region of the atmosphere) (National Research Council, 2011, p. 34). Together, these two gases help to keep the earth warm enough for life to exist (Berkman, 2002, p. 124-127). H_2O in the clouds provides rainwater that enables plants and animals to drink and CO_2 in the atmosphere enables plants to breathe. This in turn makes photosynthesis possible thus enabling animals to eat.

But the concentration of carbon dioxide is increasing exponentially along with the explosion of human population as fossil fuels such as coal and oil are burned. And the greenhouse effect is one contributing factor to the global warming that made the 20th century the warmest in the past millennium (Berkman, 2002, p. 138, 157, 207).

The climate of Antarctica and the Southern Ocean is variable due to interactions between the atmosphere, the ice, and the ocean. "This makes detection of a signal due to increasing greenhouse concentrations difficult" (Scientific Committee on Antarctic Research, 2015). If concentrations of greenhouse gases continue to increase, so too will ocean acidification. And this will likely have an adverse impact on marine life (Turner et al, 2014, p. 5).

Earth's Orbit, Wobble, and Tilt

The advance and retreat of ice sheets over the ages is associated with the eccentricity of the earth's orbit around the sun, the obliquity of the earth's axis, and the precession of equinoxes (Berkman, 2002, p. 95-97).

Every 100,000 years, the eccentricity (or lopsidedness) of the Earth's elliptical orbit is at its maximum distance from the sun (at its aphelion). And a distant sun results in a cold Earth.

Every 40,000 years, the obliquity (or tilt) of the earth's axis away from the plane of its orbit varies between 22.1° and 24.5° (averaging approximately 23.5°). And more direct sunlight produces more summer heat (Earth Observatory, 2017b).

Every 23,000 years, there is a precession (or movement) of the equinoxes when the Earth (at its perihelion) is closest to the sun, in either June or December. This is due to the gyroscopic motion of the earth on its axis similar to the wobbling of a spinning top. And a closer sun results in a warmer earth.

Ozone Layer

The ozone layer in the atmosphere absorbs harmful ultraviolet radiation from the sun that would otherwise damage exposed organisms including humans living on the surface of the earth. From

1957 to 1983, there was a 40% increase in the size of the springtime hole in the ozone layer over Antarctica. The decrease in ozone, O_3, was attributed to an increase in chlorofluorocarbon released into the atmosphere as a refrigerant in air conditioners, as a propellant in aerosols, and as a solvent.

In 1987, an international treaty was signed to phase out the production of CFC. And the Antarctic ozone hole stopped growing in 2014 (Scientific Committee on Antarctic Research, 2015, p. 4). But this same ozone hole has for years prevented large parts of the continent from warming. And, as the ozone layer recovers, it is estimated that the average temperature on the continent will increase by several degrees and that the sea ice around the continent will decrease by about a third (Howkins, 2011, p. 182, 190, 193-194).

Solar Activity

Every 11 years and at other intervals, there are changes in solar radiation. The solar cycle in the 21st century is very weak just as it was in the 17th century during the Maunder Minimum. And low sunspot activity may once again result in cooler temperatures and thus the end of the Modern Maximum (National Research Council, 2011, p. 92) and Global Warming.

Volcanic Eruptions

Volcanic activity can produce warmer weather since "the molten core of the earth has temperatures above 5000°C, which is nearly as hot as the sun" (Berkman, 2002, p. 9). And eruptions produce huge quantities of CO_2 that blanket and warm the earth. But volcanic activity can also produce cooler weather since volcanic ash reduces the amount of sunlight reaching the earth (Harpp, 2002).

Polar Effects

Polar effects are evident in the various states of water. H_2O is found in the atmosphere as a vapor, in the ocean as a liquid, and in ice sheets as a solid. In polar regions, it falls as snow and is compacted into ice on land that later melts into the sea. But "climate impacts are asymmetric around the Earth with ice sheets retreating earlier and more massively in the northern hemisphere than around Antarctica" (Berkman, 2002, p. 78, 111, 103). And "in stark contrast to the rapid warming of the Arctic, Antarctica and the

Southern Ocean present a mixed picture" (National Research Council, 2011, p. 33).

Antarctic Effects

The ice sheets of Antarctica, with ten times more ice than the rest of the earth, are divided into three major components: the Antarctic Peninsula, West Antarctica, and East Antarctica (Rodger, 2013, p. 304). Over the past 50 years, winter temperatures on the peninsula have risen 4°C but have remained more or less constant in the rest of Antarctica (Rodger, 2013, p. 302). Although West Antarctica is a little warmer during both winter and spring, the largest portion of the continent, East Antarctica, shows little change (National Research Council, 2011, p. 38).

Over the past 50 years, average annual temperature for 96% of the continent has not increased. But for the remaining 4%, on the Antarctic Peninsula, it has increased by 3°C, ten times faster than the world average (Joyner, 2013, p. 116). Over the past 50 years, 87% of 244 glaciers on the Peninsula have retreated. And, over the past 25 years, 40% of the sea ice off the Peninsula has melted (Joyner, 2013, p. 116).

The rise in water temperature west of the Antarctic Peninsula is the highest on record in the Paleolithic period of the past 10,000 years. Sea ice there has decreased 6.8% per decade since satellite observation began in 1979. Prevailing winds have contributed to a reduction of sea ice in this area but they have also contributed to an increase in other areas.

Sea ice in the Ross Sea has increased 4.5% per decade during the same period. And overall there has been a 1.0% per decade increase in sea ice around the continent (Rodger, 2013, p. 312). Antarctic sea ice has increased by an average of 18,900 square km per year since satellite observations began in 1979. And it has now "reached a new record high" (Ramsayer, 2014).

Antarctic sea ice is steadily increasing while Arctic sea ice is rapidly decreasing. But climate models tend to predict a moderate decrease in both regions. This implies that there are systemic errors and biases in these simulations (Rosenblum and Eisenman, 2016, p. 1, 6). A possible omitted variable bias (OVB) may have to do with the wind.

The Antarctic Oscillation influences the extent of sea ice. It is a see-sawing atmospheric mass between the South Pole and mid-latitudes with changing wind speed and direction. The strengthening of the westerlies isolates much of the continent and tends to have an overall cooling effect. It causes however dramatic warming on the Antarctic Peninsula as warmer air above the oceans to the north is drawn southward (Earth Observatory, 2017a).

Antarctic Relations

The Superpowers

Both Russia and the United States reserve the right to make claims in Antarctica based on their historic explorations. And neither country has recognized the Antarctic claims of other nations. Russia and the US are "the two largest players in the Antarctic ... (and) 'effectively occupy' areas ... valued due to their scientific, economic, and political importance ... (with) permanent stations and field bases ... regular voyages ... flights and traverses" (Gan, 2013, p. 136).

The Russians run rings around the continent with their stations and the Americans make themselves the center of attention with their station at the Geographic South Pole. And critics complain that the Antarctic Treaty System "remains effectively a select club dominated by the claimant states and the Cold War warriors (the US and Russia)" (Dodds and Hemmings, 2013, p. 1440).

The Anglosphere

The Antarctic Anglosphere consists of four nations. The first three are claimant nations: the UK in 1908, New Zealand in 1923, and Australia in 1933. They are listed chronologically here since they are also the first claimants of Antarctic territory. The fourth nation of the Antarctic Anglosphere is the United States, a semi-claimant nation. It is of course the hegemon not only in Antarctica but also in the rest of the world.

English is "the common language of Antarctic governance meetings" (Brady, 2013, p. 37). And critics point to "the dominant western and particularly Anglophone framing that has driven Antarctic and regional governance" (Dodds and Hemmings, 2013, p. 1435). But English is the lingua franca of the world not just Antarctica. Anglo nations are also counted among the richest nations in the world. So their influence in Antarctic is not surprising.

The Bi-Polar Nations

There are three bi-polar nations in Antarctica. One is a claimant nation, Norway. The other two are only semi-claimants, the US and Russia. But both are world superpowers. All three of these nations are coastal nations of the Arctic Ocean. They therefore have territorial seas, contiguous zones, exclusive economic zones, continental shelves, and extended continental shelves in the Arctic. And these three bi-polar nations have far more polar experience than uni-polar nations operating in just one region.

The French

France is the only claimant nation having a station outside its own sector and that station is a joint station. Non-claimant nations build and operate their own facilities under their own flags regardless of territorial claims. "Counting 110 current main facilities … only two … are joint stations, and both involve only two states (Elzinga, 2013, p. 209-210, 212).

The French and Italian station, Concordia, is located at Dome C on the Antarctic Plateau in the Australian sector. The Chilean and

German station, Bernado-O'Higgins, is located at the tip of the Antarctic Peninsula in the sector claimed first by the British, second by the Chileans, and third by the Argentines.

The Latin Neighbors

Argentina and Chile are both claimants to Antarctic territory but their claims overlap not only each other but also the earlier claim of Britain, hence the ABC dispute. Chile defends its claim based on "the papal bulls of Pope Alexnader VI (1493) and the treaty of Tordesillas (1494), which together divided the unexplored world – including any lands that might be found to the far south – between Spain and Portugal" (Klotz, 1990, p. 9-10).

Argentina also defends its claim based on these historic, some would say antiquated, rights. But both nations have somewhat stronger claims based on their proximity to the Antarctic Peninsula. Both Argentina and Chile are much closer to the continent than other nations. And both defend their Antarctic claims based on geologic as well as geographic contiguity. The tip of South America is connected geologically to the Antarctic Peninsula by the Scotia Arc, a former land bridge between the continents.

The Gateway States

There are five Gateway States to the Southern Ocean as shown on the physical map of Antarctica found at the website of Nations Online Project (2016). Listed clockwise from 0° longitude, the Greenwich Meridian, they are: South Africa, Australia, New Zealand, Chile, and Argentina. All are Consultative Parties to the Antarctic Treaty. And all are members of CCAMLR and the Madrid Protocol.

But South Africa is approximately 4000 km from the continent of Antarctica, the most distant of the five. New Zealand is approximately 3000 km away and Australia is approximately 2500 km away. And even the closest states, Chile and Argentina, are approximately 1000 km away from the continent (Antarctic Geological Drilling, 2016).

The narrowest separation between the Gateway States and Antarctica is the Drake Passage. And the tip of South America is connected to the tip of the Antarctic Peninsula by the Scotia Arc of islands. Both Argentina and Chile cite this geographical proximity as a basis for their territorial claims in Antarctica (Beck, 1986, p. 11-12).

Four of the five Gateway Nations are claimants to Antarctic territory (South Africa is not). But the suspension of claims under the Antarctic Treaty inhibits them from exercising their coastal authority over territorial seas, contiguous zones, exclusive economic zones, continental shelves, and extended continental shelves (United Nations, 2016b).

And, since there are high seas between Antarctica and all five the five Gateway States including both Argentina and Chile, their offshore authority with regard to Antarctica is as limited under the United Nations Convention on the Law of the Sea (UNCLOS) as it is under the Antarctic Treaty.

Other Nations

Developing nations have long charged developed nations with the "'appropriation of global resources" particularly by raising the "Question of Antarctica" in the UN General Assembly (Hemmings, 2012, p. 86). But few developing nations have demonstrated any interest in the continent beyond rhetorical interest. Very few of these nations have conducted any research and only a few are parties to the Antarctic Treaty (Secretariat to the Antarctic Treaty, 2016d).

"The rise of Asia, especially China and India … is … finding its due place … in the governance … of Antarctica" (Chaturvedi, 2013, p. 51). India became a Consultative Party to the Antarctic Treaty in 1983 and China in 1985. Neither have signed the CCAS (to protect seals) but both are members of CCAMLR and both have signed the Madrid Protocol (Secretariat of the Antarctic Treaty, 2016d).

China has already given Chinese names to over 350 places around the continent. And its Antarctic spending has grown from $20 million to $55 million in a decade (Economist, 2015). "If China builds all five planned stations it will have more than either Britain or Australia, an only one fewer than America" (Economist, 2013).

"The objective of demilitarizing Antarctica and its adjacent waters is achieved by the Antarctic Treaty … (but) may be threatened … by strategic competition within a multipolar world, particularly between China and India as rising powers … new regional sea powers … (and) nuclear states" (Bateman, 2012, p. 116, 120).

"Rising powers such as China, India, and South Korea are rapidly expanding their Antarctic budgets and research programs" (Brady, 2013, p. 6). South Korea "has strong … interests in Antarctica, as well as the Arctic" and since it is "poor in natural resources" much of its "research is focused on locating economically exploitable resources" (Brady and Kim, 2013, p. 75, 82, 85). South Korea has been a Consultative Party to the Antarctic Treaty since 1989. Although it has not signed the CCAS, it is a member of CCAMLR and it has signed the Madrid Protocol.

Japan is an economically stagnant power but a power nonetheless. And it has been a Consultative Party longer than any other Asian nation (if the USSR, now the Russian Federation, is considered separately as Eurasian). Japan was one of the original signatories to the Antarctic Treaty in 1961. And since then it has signed the CCAS, become a member of CCAMLR, and signed the Madrid Protocol.

But Japan's "scientific whaling" in the Southern Ocean has become increasingly controversial. Australia has repeatedly questioned the legitimacy of the Japanese research program with regard to the International Convention for the Regulation of Whaling. And, in 2008, the Federal Court of Australia found that whales were in fact taken by the Japanese in the Australian Whale Sanctuary. But this ruling has not deterred Japan's whaling activities in the region (Rothwell, Scott, and Hemmings, 2013, p. 14) (Rothwell, 2013, p. 46-47, 148).

China, India, South Korea, Japan, and Malaysia belong to the Asian Forum for Polar Sciences and its scope includes Antarctica (Elzinga, 2013, p. 203). AFoPs was formed in 2004 (Asian Forum for Polar Sciences, 2016). And it is becoming increasingly clear that Asian nations are interested in the Antarctic in general and the Southern Ocean in particular.

Antarctica may be called the white continent since it is mostly covered by ice and snow and/or since it is mostly claimed by Europeans. But sometimes the snow "has a pink, red, orange, green, yellow, or grey cast, caused by snow algae" (Rubin, 2008, p. 269). And sometimes there are lots of people in and around Antarctica besides Europeans. There are increasing numbers of staff members, scientists, and tourists as well as increasing numbers of business people engaged in prospecting for minerals and fishing. And they come from all parts of the world.

Conclusion

NGOs and the ATS

"Non-state actors such as the Antarctic and Southern Ocean Coalition have a long-standing interest and history of intervention in Antarctic diplomacy and politics" (Chaturvedi, 2012, p. 259). The ASOC was founded in 1978 and granted observer status within the Antarctic Treaty System in 1991. It lobbied against CRAMRA and for Madrid Protocol to prevent any commercial drilling or mining (Antarctic and Southern Ocean Coalition, 2016b). 26 NGOs from 10 nations were dues paying members as of 2013 (Antarctic and Southern Ocean Coalition, 2016a).

The Council of Managers of National Antarctic Programs was founded in 1988. All 29 Consultative Parties to the Antarctic Treaty are members plus one non-Consultative Party, Belarus. The purpose of COMNAP is to promote best practices with respect to scientific research. And their website provides public access to information on Antarctic facilities operated by its members (Council of Managers of National Antarctic Programs, 2016a).

The Antarctic Ocean Alliance is a more recent coalition of environmental and conservation organizations. The AOA was founded in 2010. Its sixteen "partner organizations" include the ASOC (Antarctic Ocean Alliance, 2016). And, generally speaking, all private organizations interested in Antarctica have enjoyed "much more liberal access to the Consultative Meetings" since the Rules of Procedure were revised in 1992 (Herr, 1996a, p. 108).

Most non-governmental organizations (NGOs) focus on the conservation of resources whereas most national and multinational corporations (MNCs) focus on the development of resources. Most countries also focus in one direction or the other, on either conservation or development. And they tend to advocate one policy or the other in Antarctica whether or not they have signed the Antarctic Treaty. But some of the countries that focus on development are more interested in distribution than production.

The G-77 and the ATS

Not surprisingly, least developed nations generally focus on distribution whereas developed nations generally focus on production. The LDNs are organized in the UN as the Group of 77.

And the G-77 countries typically make demands for a share of others' profits while ignoring others' losses. In short, they are advocates of a global welfare state.

They claim that outer space, the upper atmosphere, the high seas, and Antarctica are global commons (Beck, 1986, p. 278). And, since such areas are for public not private use, they insist on regulation by the United Nations as opposed to individual nations. This is convenient for the G-77 since it now has 134 members, a majority of the 193 members of the UN (The Group of 77, 2016) (United Nations, 2016e).

Socialists, the so-called workers of the world, are superficially aligned with environmentalists, the so-called the tree huggers of the world. This is true even with regard to polar politics despite the ugly facts of the matter. There is no proletariat and there are no forests on the Antarctic continent or in the Arctic Ocean. Red remains green at least on the surface but differences appear with just a scratch regardless of the location.

Green groups typically focus not only on the curtailment of production (supply) but also the curtailment of distribution (demand) due to negative externalities such as pollution. They advocate controls involving considerable costs to others but little cost to themselves. And, since both water and air pollution travel indiscriminately across national borders, they maintain that international regulation of the global commons is required.

But global regulation and taxation cannot solve the problems of poverty and pollution. The tragedy of communism and the tragedy of the commons can only be avoided by recognizing private property and national sovereignty. Self-interest and national interest are conducive to both competition and stewardship not simply one or the other. And cultural and/or regional cooperation where interests are aligned makes more sense than multi-cultural and global government where interests are diverse.

There is a widely held belief that the sun revolves around the earth. There is another widely held belief that a tradeoff exists between economic and environmental performance. These theories are logical but untrue, i.e., unsupported by the evidence. For example, non-Muslim nations do better than Muslim nations with respect to the environment and the economy. Likewise, non-African nations do better than African nations with respect to the economy and the environment. And the G-77 is representative of both Muslim and African nations.

A better economy and a better environment go hand in hand. Among all nations, the correlation between economic and environmental performance is positive .528. The real tradeoff is between human fertility on the one hand and a better economy and environment on the other. The correlation between fertility and economic performance is negative .431 and the correlation between fertility and environmental performance is negative .817. And Muslim and African countries have much higher fertility rates than non-Muslim and non-African countries. The Muslim mean is 3.96 compared to the non-Muslim mean of 2.65 and the African mean is 4.76 compared to the non-African mean of 2.33 (Craig, 2011, p. 50, 46).

The Malthusian dilemma of the 21st century is the same as it was in the 18th century: population tends to increase in a geometric ratio whereas subsistence tends to increase in an arithmetic ratio (Matlthus, 1798). Even if it is politically incorrect to speak of overpopulation in Malthusian terms, "resource-related considerations are clearly among the factors that underpin all states' interests in the Antarctic continent" (Foster, 2012, p. 154).

This is true not only for developing nations with rapidly growing populations. It is also true for developing nations with rapidly growing economies including most prominently Brazil, China, and India. Developing nations of both types are having a profound and negative impact on environmental pollution and climate change (Chaturvedi, 2012, p. 263).

Antarctic nations should flatly reject the Common Heritage of Mankind and firmly resist rent-seeking by any nation or group of nations. And they should resist any expansion of the International Seabed Authority (ISA) from the ocean to the land (International Seabed Authority, 2016b).

"It is clear that the Consultative parties do not recognize Antarctica as Common Heritage of Mankind" (Bastmeijer, 2011, p. 3). Countries and groups of countries that cannot manage their own affairs properly should not be permitted to manage the affairs of

181

others. And their governments should not be rewarded for economic and/or environmental incompetence.

In 1982, President Reagan thwarted the redistribution of wealth from the United States to the G-77. Although he supported the UN Convention on the Law of the Sea with respect to freedom of navigation, he refused to sign the UNCLOS due to its provisions with regard to deep seabed mining (Heritage Foundation, 2016).

The G-77 countries want the "international seabed to be as large as possible … (since) coastal states are required to make monetary payments or payments in kind through the International Seabed Authority (ISA) for distribution to all state parties to the LOS Convention with respect to the exploitation of nonliving seabed resources" (Riddell-Dixon, 2011, p. 377).

The twelve original signatories to the Antarctic Treaty should flatly reject a World Park and firmly resist the de-growth stance of green groups. And they should specifically resist policies advocated by groups such as the Worldwatch Institute that would punish 1st World countries for doing well economically and environmentally and reward 3rd World countries for doing poorly (Assadourian, 2012).

There are no national parks in Antarctica since national claims are held in abeyance by the Antarctic Treaty. But there are Antarctic Specially Protected Areas that no one may enter without a permit (Rubin, 2008, p. 99). At present, there are no permanent residents on the continent (Discovering Antarctica, 2015). And animals there are still unafraid of people (Rubin, 2008, p. 15, 19).

Some complain that biodiversity is not sufficiently protected since "only" 55 of 73 ASPAs are in ice-free areas (Shaw et al, 2014, p. 3). But the Antarctic region including the surrounding Southern Ocean remains one of the world's last frontiers (National Research Council, 2011, p. 1). Unfortunately, it is no longer isolated from the global political mainstream (Dodds, 2010, p. 110).

"Developments in Treaty cooperation have been substantially affected by relations to non-members" (Stokke and Vidas, 1996, p. 1). "Nations outside the Treaty are not bound by its provisions" (Chown et al, 2012, p. 158). And the wave of accessions to the Antarctic Treaty has been challenging as well (Vidas, 1996a, p. 56-57). Whereas there were 12 Consultative Parties to the Treaty in 1959, there are 29 today. And now there are also 24 non-

Consultative Parties invited to attend the Consultative Meetings (Secretariat of the Antarctic Treaty, 2016d).

The growth in membership increases the potential for a breakdown in the consensus that characterizes the Antarctic Treaty System (Klotz, 1990, 114). And it is possible that some of the new parties to the Antarctic Treaty intend to destroy the club from within (Beck, 1986, p. 199). What will happen if the Antarctic Treaty System "breaks down, or its fundamentals are attacked" (Haward, 2012, p. 236).

At present, the ATS "is confronted with both a complex, crowded, and compelling agenda ... and a marked decline in its overall capacity to effectively deliberate and deliver legally binding measures ... a situation insightfully termed as 'hollowing of Antarctic governance'" (Chaturvedi, 2012, p. 257). And any "regulation of Antarctic activities by external regimes or organizations creates the risk that the ATS is more generally undermined" (Scott, 2012, p. 296-297).

Both socialists and capitalists are critical of the ATS. But whereas the former support more regulation and taxation, the latter support more freedom. This is true with respect to both the environment and the economy. Environmental NGOs and the less developed countries represented by the G77 typically favor a wider and deeper approach to government. MNCs and the more developed countries represented by the OECD typically favor a narrower and shallower approach (Organization for Economic Cooperation and Development, 2016).

The Antarctic Treaty System operates in a capitalist laissez faire fashion on the assumption that activities are permitted unless prohibited (Herr, 1996b, p. 207, 223) and not in a socialist command and control fashion on the assumption that activities are prohibited unless permitted. The ATS is "a framework for a limited system of administration in Antarctic affairs" (Klotz, 1990, p. 36).

But the ATS "breaks with the fixity of legal concepts, in going beyond the freedom-sovereignty-commons trichotomy" (Vidas, 1996b, p. 71). Its resource regimes make no distinction between claimed and unclaimed sectors nor between territorial waters and high seas. It is a regional system as opposed to national or global. And "there is a very obvious difficulty ... in the belief of seven claimants plus the semi-claimants of the United States and Russia that they have … sovereignty rights" (Hemmings, 2014, p. 7).

Both CAMMLR and Madrid Protocol apply all the way to the outer limit of the Antarctic Convergence that wanders between 60° S and 50° S. This is beyond the boundary of the Antarctic Treaty at 60° S and well beyond the Arctic Circle at 66°33′ S. "Competing security concerns … may … become seeds of conflict … and unresolved territorial claims may … threaten Antarctic regime security" (Nasu, 2012, p. 32, 29). And "it may be expected that conflicts will arise between ATS states and states outside the ATS" (Bastmeijer, 2011, p. 37).

Many outsiders view the Antarctic Treaty "as an act of imperialism" albeit one that is regarded as post-colonial due to the "distinction between formal and effective sovereignty" (Scott, 2011). But "sovereign neutrality" is fundamental to the operation of the Antarctic Treaty System. The concept is deliberately ambiguous to accommodate the divergent positions of states that are parties to the Treaty. The Treaty should not however "be interpreted as a renunciation of previously asserted rights" (Triggs, 2011, p. 43).

Due to growing confusion and diminishing respect, it may be time to abandon the Treaty altogether. It may be time to reassert national sovereignty and the original claims to Antarctic territory by the UK in 1908, New Zealand in 1923, France in 1924, Australia in 1933, and Norway in 1939. And it may be time for Norway to specify the extent of its claim in terms of latitude (Joyner, 1998, p. 17). It may also be time to resolve the disputed claims by Chile in 1940 and Argentina in 1943.

And finally it may be time for the United States and Russia to renounce any claims to Antarctica as a whole and simply split the unclaimed portion of the continent. Long ago, Chilean officials wisely cautioned that any new claims "beyond the unclaimed sector from 90° W to 150° W would provoke animosity rather than cooperation" (Moore, 2001, p. 736).

The unclaimed sector is 16.66% (one sixth) of the fifth largest continent in the world (Antarctic Geological Drilling, 2016). Half of that is 8.33% (one twelfth) or 1,166,200 square km out of 14 million square km. That land area is almost as large as the 1,477,953 square km of Alaska that Russia sold to the United States in 1867 (U.S. Geological Survey, 2016).

And now that US President Obama has been replaced by President Trump, a real estate tycoon, it may be easier to make the Deal of the Century with Russian Federation President Putin. But opponents of Trump and/or Putin may be expected to ridicule such a deal. Present-day naysayers may even call it Tillerson's Folly, after the new US Secretary of State, just as latter-day naysayers called it Seward's Folly, after the old one (U.S. Office of the Historian, 2016).

Meanwhile, in the absence of traditional territorial sovereignty, economic development remains compromised in Antarctica due to the strict regulation of prospecting and production. And "in the absence of traditional coastal state jurisdiction … environment security … remains compromised" in the Southern Ocean due to the lax regulation of pollution (Rothwell, 2012b, p. 145).

Reassertion of the original Antarctic claims would most certainly entail dissolution of the existing Antarctic Treaty (Joyner, 2002, p. 47). But that could quite possibly lead to the creation of a Southern

Ocean Treaty Organization (SOTO) along the lines of the North Atlantic Treaty Organization (NATO).

The original North Atlantic Treaty Organization with a limited number of members (12 compared to 28 now) provides a good model (North Atlantic Treaty Organization, 2016a). NATO's "purpose is to safeguard the freedom and security of its members though political and military means" (North Atlantic Treaty Organization, 2016b). Such an alliance would facilitate regional competition and cooperation on both economic and environmental matters.

Such an alliance would be less ambitious but more practical than a South Atlantic Treaty Organization (SATO) (Hurrell, 1983) with distant and diverse members. It would also eliminate the contentious categories of membership under the existing Antarctic Treaty. The procedure for withdrawal from the Antarctic Treaty is outlined in Article XII (2) (National Science Foundation, 2016).

Regional coordination by the nine Antarctic claimants would be the best way to promote economic development and to insure environmental protection in the short term. In the long run, "deconstruction of the nation-state" and "disaggregation of the mixed political economy" would be even better (Craig, 2010b, p. 414).

Government power could eventually shift upwards to global organizations as socialism is employed to alleviate the pollution of water and air. And market power could eventually shift downwards to local governments as capitalism is employed to alleviate the poverty of individuals.

But transition to this New World Order (NWO) could take quite some time. In the meantime, it is up to national governments to claim complete sovereignty over their southernmost territories, territorial seas, contiguous zones, exclusive economic zones, continental shelves, outer continental shelves, and contiguous high seas.

And it is also up to claimant nations to collaborate with one another on a regional basis. Regional economic opportunities would stimulate competitive and cooperative economic enterprise including bioprospecting, tourism, fishing, drilling, and mining. And regional environmental threats would stimulate competitive and cooperative environmental stewardship (Craig, 2016).

Claims by the Antarctic 9 mirror those by the Arctic 5. The southern group consists of Argentina, Australia, Chile, France, New Zealand, Norway, Russia, the UK, and the US. And the northern group consists of Canada, Denmark (by virtue of Greenland), Norway, Russia, and the US (by virtue of Alaska).

The Antarctic 9 and the Artic 5 have the proximate incentive as well as the immediate ability to simultaneously exploit and protect the polar regions. They also have an opportunity to develop best practices that would serve as good examples in other parts of the world by formulating new Antarctic and Arctic agreements that involve not only deregulated and untaxed trade but also regulated and taxed pollution.

These 14 nations could easily find common cause in resisting the claims of other nations, environmental interest groups, and international organizations such as the UN. China in particular "looms as a major power with global interests … (and) is extremely interested in the resources of both Antarctica and the Arctic"

(Bateman, 2012, p. 119, 123). "Like previous geographies of the imperial and Cold War eras, new global geographies are likely to emerge (Dean, Naylor, Turchetti, and Siegert, 2008, p. 595).

"The Cold War is over" (Collis, 2010, p. 394). But a New Cold War, perhaps termed a Real Cold War, may be even more polarizing than the Old Cold War. Instead of pitting the US versus the USSR as in the Last Cold War, the Next Cold War could pit the US and Russia along with their polar allies against a majority of other nations including China and India. Yet even a Real Cold War need not entail bloody conflict since economic development and environmental protection of the polar regions by polar nations would be beneficial to mankind in general.

It is important to remember that the US and Russia are still superpowers. Cooperation between them remains essential to the peace and stability of the world. Like Norway, they have a national interest to protect in both the Antarctic and the Arctic. And, since the seasons are reversed in the southern and northern hemispheres, bipolar nations are able to use the same ships and planes in both regions by moving them back and forth to take advantage of longer days and warmer weather year 'round (Belanger, 2006, p. 18).

The languages of the superpowers are already common in the region. This is true even if English takes precedence over Russian not only due to its acceptance as a new lingua franca but also due to the polar involvement of Commonwealth nations: Australia, New Zealand, and the UK in the Antarctic; and, Canada in the Arctic.

Russia is the largest country in the world in terms of area but America and the other Anglo countries are among the richest. And this wealth combined with the ubiquity of the English language may be enough to persuade Russia to join either a Southern Ocean Treaty Organization or an Arctic Ocean Treaty Organization or even a north-south Polar Treaty Organization.

The Common Heritage of Mankind involves a grand paradox. Common space simultaneously belongs to everyone (res communis) and to no one (res nullius) (Peterson, 1998, p. 36) (Joyner, 1998, p. 33). These antithetical policies inevitably result in the tragedy of communism (economic depression) and the tragedy of the commons (environmental devastation).

"The state remains the basic unit of the modern international order" (Herr, 1996a, p. 93). "National interest has always superseded global interest … (and) it is in the national interest of every coastal state to foster economic development and to insure environmental protection off its shores" as well as on its shores (Craig, 2010a, p. 25).

The sovereignty of coastal nations on the southern shores of the Southern Ocean is as important as the sovereignty of coastal nations on the southern shores of the Arctic Ocean. And the sovereignty of polar nations is as important as the sovereignty of nations anywhere else in the world. Anything less would constitute a legal double standard violating the principal of equal protection under the law.

The Antarctic is a continent surrounded by an ocean. And coastal nations there have adopted a more legalistic hard-law approach in the form of the Antarctic Treaty. The Arctic is an ocean surrounded by continents. And coastal nations there have adopted a less legalistic soft-law approach in the form of an Artic Council (Koivurova, 2005, p. 213-214). But regardless of the approach, each coastal nation is pursuing what it perceives to be in its national interest.

The realist school of international relations is now in session. And it is time for an "international discussion in pursuit of Antarctic policies that will embrace both human and environmental concerns" (Foster, 2012, p. 155). But the discussion should be confined to nations with legitimate claims to Antarctic territory based on original exploration and occupation of the continent.

References

Antarctic Geological Drilling (2016). *All about Antarctica.*
http://www.andrill.org/about/antarctica

Antarctic Ocean Alliance (2016). *Supporters.*
http://www.antarcticocean.org/supporters/

Antarctic and Southern Ocean Coalition (2016a). *ASOC Council:*
Dues paying members.
http://www.asoc.org/storage/documents/ASOC_Council_List
111513.pdf

Antarctic and Southern Ocean Coalition (2016b). *History of the*
Antarctic and Southern Ocean Coalition.
http://www.asoc.org/about/history

Antarctic and Southern Ocean Coalition (2016c). *Southern Ocean*
Whale Sanctuary. http://www.asoc.org/advocacy/antarctic-
wildlife-conservation/southern-ocean-whale-sanctuary

Asian Forum for Polar Sciences (2016). *Who are we?*
http://afops.org/m11.php

Assadourian, E. (2012). The path to degrowth in overdeveloped
countries. *State of the World 2012: Moving Toward*
Sustainable Prosperity.
http://www.worldwatch.org/system/files/SOW12%20Summa
ry%20%28Chapter%202%29.pdf

Australian Antarctic Division (2016a). *Antarctic Weather*.
http://www.antarctica.gov.au/about-antarctica/environment/weather

Australian Antarctic Division (2016b). The *Madrid Protocol.*
http://www.antarctica.gov.au/law-and-treaty/the-madrid-protocol

Australian Antarctic Division (2016c). *Poles and directions*.
http://www.antarctica.gov.au/about-antarctica/environment/geography/poles-and-directions

Australian Antarctic Division (2016d). *Sunlight hours*.
http://www.antarctica.gov.au/about-antarctica/environment/weather/sunlight-hours

Australian Antarctic Division (2016e). *What is the Southern Ocean?*
http://www.antarctica.gov.au/magazine/2001-2005/issue-4-spring-2002/feature2/what-is-the-southern-ocean

Basberg, B. (2010). Antarctic tourism and maritime heritage. *International Journal of Maritime History*, XXII(2), 227-246.

Basken, P. (2012). U.S. Antarctic science is at a crossroads as the wider world presses in. *Chronicle of Higher Education*, February 12, 2012).

Bastmeijer, K. (2011). Intergenerational equity and the Antarctic Treaty System: Continued efforts to prevent "mastery". *Yearbook of Polar Law*, 3(1).

Bateman, S. (2012). Strategic competition and emerging security risks. In A.D. Hemmings, D.R. Rothwell, & Scott, K.N. (Eds.), *Antarctic Security in the Twenty-First Century: Legal and Policy Perspectives* (pp. 116-134). New York: Routledge.

Beck, P. (1986). *The International Politics of Antarctica.* London: Croom Helm.

Belanger, D.O. (2006). *Deep Freeze: The United States, the International Geophysical Year, and the Origins of Antarctica's Age of Science*. Boulder, CO: University Press of Colorado.

Berkman, P.A. (2002). *Science into Policy: Global Lessons from Antarctica*. London: Academic Press.

Berkman, P.A. (2009). Antarctic Treaty Summit: Science-policy interactions in international governance. In Alfredsson, G., Koivurova, T., & Leary, D.K. (Eds). *Yearbook of Polar Law*, Vol. 1, pp. 511- 525.

Berkman, P.A., Lang, M.A. Walton, D.W.H. & Young, O.R. (2011). *Science Diplomacy: Antarctica, Science, and the Governance of International Spaces*. Washington, DC: Smithsonian Institution Scholarly Press.

Brady, A. (Ed.) (2013). *The Emerging Politics of Antarctica*. New York: Routledge.

Brady, A. (2013). China's Antarctic interests. In A. Brady (Ed.), *The Emerging Politics of Antarctica* (pp. 31-49). New York: Routledge.

Brady, A. (2013). New Zealand's Antarctica. In A. Brady (Ed.), *The Emerging Politics of Antarctica* (pp. 147-162). New York: Routledge.

Brady, A. & S. Kim (2013). Cool Korea: Korea's growing Antarctic interests. In A. Brady (Ed.), *The Emerging Politics of Antarctica* (pp. 75-95). New York: Routledge.

British Antarctic Survey (2016). *Antarctic Overview Map.* National Aeronautics and Space Administration: Landsat Image Mosaic of Antarctica. http://lima.nasa.gov/pdf/A3_overview.pdf

Cassano, J.J. (2013). Climate of extremes. In D.W.H. Walton (Ed.), *Antarctica: Global Science from a Frozen Continent* (pp. 102-136). Cambridge University Press.

Center for International Earth Science Information Network (2016). *Agreed Measures for the Conservation of Antarctic Fauna and Flora.* Environmental Treaties and Resource Indicators. http://sedac.ciesin.org/entri/texts/acrc/aff64.txt.html

Chaturvedi, S. (2012). The Antarctic 'climate security' dilemma and the future of Antarctic governance. In A.D. Hemmings, D.R. Rothwell, & Scott, K.N. (Eds.), *Antarctic Security in the Twenty-First Century: Legal and Policy Perspectives* (pp. 257-283). New York: Routledge.

Chaturvedi, S. (2013). India and Antarctica: Towards post-colonial engagement? In A. Brady (Ed.), *The Emerging Politics of Antarctica* (pp. 50-74). New York: Routledge.

Chown, S.L., et al (2012). Challenges to the future conservation of the Antarctic. *Science*, 337, 158-159.

Collis, C. (2010). Critical legal geographies of possession: Antarctica and the International Geophysical Year 1957-1958. *GeoJournal*, 75, 387-395.

Commission for the Conservation of Antarctic Marine Living Resources (2016a). *About CCAMLR*. https://www.ccamlr.org/en/organisation/about-ccamlr

Commission for the Conservation of Antarctic Marine Living Resources (2016b). *Members*. https://www.ccamlr.org/en/organisation/members

Connecticut Humanities (2016). *Nathaniel Palmer discovers Antarctica*. http://connecticuthistory.org/nathaniel-palmer-discovers-antarctica-today-in-history/

Convey, P., Brandt, A., & Nicol, S. (2013). Life in a cold environment. In D.W.H. Walton (Ed.), *Antarctica: Global Science from a Frozen Continent* (pp. 161-210). Cambridge University Press.

Convey, P. (2014). Antarctic Research: Significance to the global community. *International e-Journal Science, Medicine, & Education*, 8(3), 1-3.

Convey, P., Hughes, K.A., & Tin, T. (2012). Continental governance and environmental management mechanisms under the Antarctic Treaty System: Sufficient for the biodiversity challenges of this century? *Biodiversity, iFirst*, 1-15.

Conway, E. (2010). *Is Antarctica melting?* National Aeronautics and Space Administration/Jet Propulsion Laboratory. http://www.nasa.gov/topics/earth/features/20100108_Is_Anta rctica_Melting.html

Council of Managers of National Antarctic Programs (2016a). *About COMNAP*. https://www.comnap.aq/SitePages/Home.aspx

Council of Managers of National Antarctic Programs (2016b). *Our Members*. https://ucnz.maps.arcgis.com/apps/webappviewer/index.html ?id=8663617ffa264e45aa3804d0d08fcdf8

Craig, K. (2010a). The extension of territorial waters. *US-China Law Review*, 7(5), 15-25.

Craig, K. (2010b). The new world order: A deconstruction of the nation-state and a disaggregation of the mixed political economy. *International Journal of Public Administration*, 33(8-9), 414-420.

Craig, K. (2011). The blame game in international relations. *National Social Science Journal*, 35(2), 43-54.

Craig, K. (2016). The Arctic Frontier in International Relations. *Florida Political Chronicle*, 24(2).

Crystalinks (2017). *Earth's Magnetic Field.* http://www.crystalinks.com/earthsmagneticfield.html

Davis, R. (2007). Enforcing Australian las in Antarctica: The HIS litigation. *Melbourne Journal of International Law*, 8(1), 142-158.

Dean, K., Naylor, S., Turchetti, S., Siegert, M. (2008). Data in Antarctic science and politics. *Social Studies of Science*, 38(4), 571-604.

Diaz, D. & Keller, K. (2016). A potential disintegration of the West Antarctic Ice Sheet: Implications for economic analyses of climate policy. Papers and Proceedings, *American Economic Review*, 106(5), 607-611.

Discovering Antarctica (2015). *Antarctica: The frozen continent.* http://www.discoveringantarctica.org.uk/downloads/1_frozen _cont.pdf

Dodds, K. (2010). Governing Antarctica: Contemporary challenges and the enduring legacy of the 1959 Antarctic Treaty. *Global Policy*, 1(1), 108-115.

Dodds, K.J. (2011). Sovereignty watch: claimant states, resources, and territory in contemporary Antarctica. *Polar Record*, 47(242), 231-243.

Dodds, K. (2012). The Antarctic Peninsula: Territory, sovereignty watch and the 'Antarctic problem'. In A.D. Hemmings, D.R. Rothwell, & Scott, K.N. (Eds.), *Antarctic Security in the Twenty-First Century: Legal and Policy Perspectives* (pp. 95-115). New York: Routledge.

Dodds, K. & Hemmings, A.D. (2013). Britain and the British Antarctic Territory in the wider geopolitics of the Antarctic and the Southern Ocean. *International Affairs*, 89(6), 1429-1444.

Dudeney, J.R. & Walton, D.W.H. (2012). Leadership in politics and science within the Antarctic Treaty. *Polar Research*, 31(11075), 1-9.

Earth Observatory (2017a). *Antarctic Sea Ice.* http://earthobservatory.nasa.gov/Features/SeaIce/page4.php

Earth Observatory (2017b). *Orbital Variations.* http://earthobservatory.nasa.gov/Features/Milankovitch/milankovitch_2.php

Economist (2012, March 6). *Antarctic ecology: Polar invaders.* http://www.economist.com/blogs/babbage/2012/03/antarctic-ecology?zid=313&ah=fe2aac0b11adef572d67aed9273b6e55

Economist (2013, November 7). *China in Antarctic: Polar power play.*
http://www.economist.com/blogs/analects/2013/11/china-antarctic?zid=313&ah=fe2aac0b11adef572d67aed9273b6e55

Economist (2015, January 31). *Antarctica: Core Values.*
http://www.economist.com/news/international/21641239-southern-continent-hots-up-core-values?zid=313&ah=fe2aac0b11adef572d67aed9273b6e55

Elzinga, A. (2013). Rallying around a flag? On the persistent gap in scientific internationalism between word and deed. In A. Brady (Ed.), *The Emerging Politics of Antarctica* (pp. 193-213). New York: Routledge.

Fahrbach, E. (2013). Stormy and icy seas. In D.W.H. Walton (Ed.), *Antarctica: Global Science from a Frozen Continent* (pp. 137-160). Cambridge University Press.

Foster, C.E. (2012). Antarctic resources and human security. In A.D. Hemmings, D.R. Rothwell, & Scott, K.N. (Eds.), *Antarctic Security in the Twenty-First Century: Legal and Policy Perspectives* (pp. 154-171). New York: Routledge.

Fox, D. (2014). Lakes under the ice: Antarctica's secret garden. *Nature*, 512, 244-246. http://www.nature.com/news/lakes-under-the-ice-antarctica-s-secret-garden-1.15729

Gan, I. (2013). Russia, the post-Soviet world, and Antarctica. In A. Brady (Ed.), *The Emerging Politics of Antarctica* (pp. 130-146). New York: Routledge.

Group of 77. *About the Group of 77.* http://www.g77.org/doc/

Guyomard, A. (2010). Ethics and bioprospecting in Antarctica. *Ethics in Science and Environmental Politics*, 10, 31-44.

Hansen, T.L. (2016). *The Northern Lights: Where, when and what.* University of Tromso: Tromso Geophysical Observatory. http://geo.phys.uit.no/articl/nord_eng.html

Hamzah, B.A. (2013). The Malaysian journey to the Antarctic: a glimpse at public policy dynamics. In A. Brady (Ed.), *The Emerging Politics of Antarctica* (pp. 96-109). New York: Routledge.

Harpp, K. (2002). How do volcanoes affect world climate? *Scientific American*, April 15, 2002. https://www.scientificamerican.com/article/how-do-volcanoes-affect-w/

Haward, M. (2012). Marine resources management, security and the Antarctic Treaty System. In A.D. Hemmings, D.R. Rothwell, & Scott, K.N. (Eds.), *Antarctic Security in the Twenty-First Century: Legal and Policy Perspectives* (pp. 215-237). New York: Routledge.

Hemmings, A.D. (2010). Does bioprospecting risk moral hazard for science in the Antarctic Treaty System? *Ethics in Science and Environmental Politics*, 10, 5-12.

Hemmings, A.D. (2012). Security beyond claims. In A.D. Hemmings, D.R. Rothwell, & Scott, K.N. (Eds.), *Antarctic Security in the Twenty-First Century: Legal and Policy Perspectives* (pp. 70-94). New York: Routledge.

Hemmings, A.D. & Stephens, T. (2010). The extended continental shelves of sub-Antarctic islands: Implications for Antarctic governance. *Polar Record*, 46(239), 312-327.

Hemmings, A.D., Rothwell, D.R., & Scott, K.N. (Eds.) (2012). *Antarctic Security in the Twenty-First Century: Legal and Policy Perspectives*. New York: Routledge.

Hemmings, A.D. (2014). Re-justifying the Antarctic Treaty System for the 21st century: Rights, expectations and global equity. In R. Powell & K. Dodds (Eds.), *Polar Geopolitics: Knowledges, Resources and Legal Regimes*. Northampton, MA: Edward Elgar.

Hemmings, A.D. (2015). Antarctic Treaty System. In J. Morin & A. Orsini (Eds.), *The Companion to Global Environmental Governance*. Routledge / Earthscan.

Heritage Foundation (2016). *Why the "Law of the Sea Treaty" is still a bad idea*. http://heritageaction.com/stoplost/why-the-law-of-the-sea-treaty-is-still-a-bad-idea/

Herr, R.A. (1996a). The changing roles of non-governmental organizations in the Antarctic Treaty System. In O.S. Stokke & D. Vidas (Eds.), *Governing the Antarctic* (pp. 91-110). Cambridge: Cambridge University Press.

Herr, R.A. (1996b). The effectiveness of Antarctic tourism: A study in regime effectiveness. In O.S. Stokke & D. Vidas (Eds.), *Governing the Antarctic* (pp. 203-223). Cambridge: Cambridge University Press.

Historical Sea Ice Atlas (2016). *Glossary: Common terms used in sea ice research*. Fairbanks, AL: University of Alaska. http://seaiceatlas.snap.uaf.edu/glossary

Howard, M. (2013). The Antarctic Treaty System: Challenges, coordination, and congruity. In A. Brady (Ed.), *The Emerging Politics of Antarctica* (pp. 13-28). New York: Routledge.

Howkins, Adrian (2011). Melting empires? Climate change and politics in Antarctica since the International Geophysical Year. *History of Science Society*, 26(1), 180-197.

Hughes, K.A., & Bridge, P.D. (2010). Potential impacts of Antarctic bioprospecting and associated commercial activities upon Antarctic science and scientists. *Ethics in Science and Environmental Politics*, 10, 13-18.

Hughes, K.A. & Convey, P. (2014). Alien invasions in Antarctica – Is anyone liable? *Polar Research*, 33, 1-13.

Hughes, K.A., Lopez-Martinez, J., Francis, J.E., Crame, J.A., Carcavilla, L., Shiraishi, K., Hokada, Y., & Yamaguchi, A. (2016, February). Antarctic geoconservation: A review of current systems and practices. *Environmental Conservation*, 200, 1-12.

Hughes, K.A., & Pertierra, L.R. (2016). Evaluation of non-native species policy development and implementation within the Antarctic Treat area. *Biological Conservation*, 149-159.

Hurrell, A. (1983). The politics of South Atlantic security: A survey of proposals for a South Atlantic Treaty Organization. *International Affairs*, 59(2), 179-193.

International Association of Antarctic Tour Operators (2016). *What is IAATO?* https://iaato.org/what-is-iaato

IBCSO (2016). *International Bathometric Chart of the Southern Ocean.* http://hs.pangaea.de/Maps/bathy/IBCSO_v1/IBCSO_v1_digital_chart_pdfA.pdf

International Maritime Organization (2016a). *Brief History of IMO.* http://www.imo.org/en/About/HistoryOfIMO/Pages/Default.aspx

International Maritime Organization (2016b). *Introduction.* http://www.imo.org/en/About/Conventions/Pages/Home.aspx

International Seabed Authority (2016a). *About the International Seabed Authority.* https://www.isa.org.jm/authority

International Seabed Authority (2016b). *Mining Code.* https://www.isa.org.jm/mining-code

Isaacson, A. (2016). Into Thin Ice. *National Geographic*, 229, 1, 98-117.

Jabour, J. (2010). Biological prospecting: The ethics of exclusive reward from Antarctic activity. *Ethics in Science and Environmental Politics*, 10, 19-29.

Jabour, J. (2012). Maritime security: Investing in safe shipping operations to help prevent marine pollution. In A.D. Hemmings, D.R. Rothwell, & Scott, K.N. (Eds.), *Antarctic Security in the Twenty-First Century: Legal and Policy Perspectives* (pp. 238-256). New York: Routledge.

Jabour, J. (2013). Biological prospecting in the Antarctic. In A. Brady (Ed.), *The Emerging Politics of Antarctica* (pp. 242-257). New York: Routledge.

Joyner, C.C. (1998). *Governing the Frozen Commons: The Antarctic Regime and Environmental Protection*. University of South Carolina Press.

Joyner, C.C. (2012). Bioprospecting as a challenge to the Antarctic Treaty. In A.D. Hemmings, D.R. Rothwell, & Scott, K.N. (Eds.), *Antarctic Security in the Twenty-First Century: Legal and Policy Perspectives* (pp. 197-214). New York: Routledge.

Joyner, C.C. (2013). United States foreign policy interests in Antarctica. In A. Brady (Ed.), *The Emerging Politics of Antarctica* (pp. 110-129). New York: Routledge.

Klotz, F.G (1990). *America on the Ice: Antarctic Policy Issues.* Washington, DC: National Defense University Press.

Koivurova, T. (2005). Environmental protection in the Arctic and Antarctic: Can the polar regimes learn from each other? *International Journal of Legal Information*, 33(2), 204-218.

Koivurova, T. (2013). Multipolar and Multilevel Governance in the Arctic and the Antarctic. Proceedings of the Annual Meeting, *American Society of International Law*, 107, 443-446.

Kriwoken, L.K., Jabour, J., & Hemmings, A.D. (Eds.) (2007). *Looking South: Australia's Antarctic Agenda.* Annandale, NSW: Federation Press.

Lanzerotti, L.J. & Weatherwax, A.T. (2013). Space research from Antarctica. In D.W.H. Walton (Ed.), *Antarctica: Global Science from a Frozen Continent* (pp. 211-228). Cambridge University Press.

Lopez-Martinez, J. & Sparrow, M.D. (2014). Science in Antarctica and the role of the Scientific Committee on Antarctic Research (SCAR). *Journal of the Black Sea/Mediterranean Environment*, 20(2), 127-136.

Malthus, T. (1798). *An Essay on the Principle of Population.* London: J. Johnson http://rescuingbiomedicalresearch.org/wp-content/uploads/2015/04/Malthus-1798.pdf

Masson-Delmotte, V. (2013). Ice with everything. In D.W.H. Walton (Ed.), *Antarctica: Global Science from a Frozen Continent* (pp. 67-101). Cambridge University Press.

Moore, J.K. (2001). Maritime rivalry, political intervention and the race to Antarctica: US-Chilean relations, 1939-1949. *Journal of Latin American Studies, 33,* 713-738.

Mossop, J. (2012). The security challenge posed by scientific permit whaling and its opponents in the Southern Ocean. In A.D. Hemmings, D.R. Rothwell, & Scott, K.N. (Eds.), *Antarctic Security in the Twenty-First Century: Legal and Policy Perspectives* (pp. 307-327). New York: Routledge.

Nasu, H. (2012). Law and policy for Antarctic security. In A.D. Hemmings, D.R. Rothwell, & Scott, K.N. (Eds.), *Antarctic Security in the Twenty-First Century: Legal and Policy Perspectives* (pp. 18-32). New York: Routledge.

National Aeronautics and Space Administration (2016). *A super solar flare.* https://science.nasa.gov/science-news/science-at-nasa/2008/06may_carringtonflare

National Geographic Magazine Online (2008). *Discover Antarctica.* http://ngm.nationalgeographic.com/ngm/antarctica/

National Research Council (2011). *Future Science Opportunities in Antarctica and the Southern Ocean*. Washington, DC: National Academies Press.

National Science Foundation (2016). *The Antarctic Treaty*. https://www.nsf.gov/geo/plr/antarct/anttrty.jsp

National Snow & Ice Data Center (2016a). *All about Sea Ice*. https://nsidc.org/cryosphere/seaice/index.html

National Snow & Ice Data Center (2016b). *Arctic Sea Ice News & Analysis: Map of Antarctica*. http://nsidc.org/arcticseaicenews/map-of-antarctica/

National Snow & Ice Data Center (2106c). *Quick Facts on Icebergs*. https://nsidc.org/cryosphere/quickfacts/icebergs.html

National Snow & Ice Data Center (2016d). *Quick Facts on Ice Shelves*. https://nsidc.org/cryosphere/quickfacts/iceshelves.html

Nations Online Project (2016). *Physical Map of Antarctica*. http://www.nationsonline.org/oneworld/map/antarctica_map.htm

North Atlantic Treaty Organization (2016a). *The North Atlantic Treaty*. http://www.nato.int/cps/en/natohq/official_texts_17120.htm

North Atlantic Treaty Organization (2016b). *What is NATO?* http://www.nato.int/nato-welcome/index.html

Ohio State University (2008). *Solar Energy, Albedo, and the Polar Regions.* http://beyondpenguins.ehe.osu.edu/issue/energy-and-the-polar-environment/solar-energy-albedo-and-the-polar-regions

O'Reilly, J., Oreskes, N., & Oppenheimer, M. (2012). The rapid disintegration of projections: The West Antarctic Ice Sheet and the Intergovernmental Panel on Climate Change. *Social Studies of Science*, 42(5), 709-731.

Organization for Economic Cooperation and Development (2016). *List of OECD Member Countries.* http://www.oecd.org/about/membersandpartners/list-oecd-member-countries.htm

Orheim, O. (2013). Managing the frozen commons. In Walton, D.W.H. (Ed.) (2013). *Antarctica: Global Science from a Frozen Continent* (pp. 273-300). Cambridge: Cambridge University Press.

Peterson, M.J. (1988). *Managing the Frozen South: The Creation and Evolution of the Antarctic Treaty System.* Berkeley: University of California Press.

Phys.org (2016). New map reveals how little of Antarctica's rock is ice free. *British Antarctic Survey.* https://phys.org/news/2016-08-reveals-antarctica-ice-free.html

Plant, B. (2015). *Sovereignty, science, and cetaceans: The whaling in the Antarctic case*. Cambridge Law Journal, 74(1), 40-44.

Polar Geospatial Center (2015). *Antarctica*. University of Minnesota. http://www.pgc.umn.edu/maps/antarctic/id/ANT_REF-MP2015-001

Previdi, M., & Polvani, L.M. (2016). Anthropogenic impact on Antarctic surface mass balance, currently masked by natural variability, to emerge by mid-century. *Environmental Research Letters*, 1-9.

Ramsayer, K. (2014). *Antarctic sea ice reaches new record maximum*. National Aeronautics and Space Administration/Goddard Space Flight Center. https://www.nasa.gov/content/goddard/antarctic-sea-ice-reaches-new-record-maximum

Redgwell, C. (1999). Protection of ecosystems under international law: Lessons from Antarctica. In A.E. Boyle & D. Freestone (Eds.), *International Law and Sustainable Development: Past Achievements and Future Challenges*. Oxford University Press.

Riddell-Dixon, E. (2011). Meeting the deadline: Canada's Arctic submission to the Commission on the Limits of the Continental Shelf. *Ocean Development & International Law*, 42, 4, 368-382.

Rodger, A. (2013). Stormy and icy seas. In D.W.H. Walton (Ed.), Antarctica: *Global Science from a Frozen Continent* (pp. 301-324). Cambridge University Press.

Rosenblum, E., & Eisenman, I. (2016). Can natural variability explain the discrepancy between observed and modeled sea ice trends? *Journal of Climate*. http://eisenman.ucsd.edu/papers/Rosenblum-Eisenman-2016a.pdf

Rothwell, D.R. (2010). Sovereignty and the Antarctic Treaty. *Polar Record*, 46(1), 17-20.

Rothwell, D.R., Scott, K.N., & Hemmings, A.D. (2012). The search for Antarctic security. In A.D. Hemmings, D.R. Rothwell, & Scott, K.N. (Eds.), *Antarctic Security in the Twenty-First Century: Legal and Policy Perspectives* (pp. 1-17). New York: Routledge.

Rothwell, D.R. (2012a). The Antarctic Treaty as a security construct. In A.D. Hemmings, D.R. Rothwell, & Scott, K.N. (Eds.), *Antarctic Security in the Twenty-First Century: Legal and Policy Perspectives* (pp. 33-50). New York: Routledge.

Rothwell, D.R. (2012b). Law enforcement in Antarctica. In A.D. Hemmings, D.R. Rothwell, & Scott, K.N. (Eds.), *Antarctic Security in the Twenty-First Century: Legal and Policy Perspectives* (pp. 135-153). New York: Routledge.

Rubin, J. (2008). *Antarctica (4th ed.)*. Australia: Lonely Planet Publications.

Sanson, L. (2013). Living and working in the cold. In D.W.H. Walton (Ed.), *Antarctica: Global Science from a Frozen Continent* (pp. 229-252). Cambridge University Press.

Schuch, L.A., Garg, V.K., Kuzmann, E., Garg, R., & de Oliveira, A.C. (2001). Antarctica: General Aspects and Brazilian research activities. *Environmental Management and Health*, 12(1), 67-78.

Scientific Committee on Antarctic Research (2015). *Antarctic Climate Change and the Environment – 2015Update*. http://www.scar.org/scar_media/documents/policyadvice/trea typapers/ATCM38_ip092_e.pdf

Scientific Committee on Antarctic Research (2016a). *About us.* http://www.scar.org/about-us

Scientific Committee on Antarctic Research (2016b). *History.* http://www.scar.org/about/history

Scott, K.N. (2012). Scientific rhetoric and Antarctic security. In A.D. Hemmings, D.R. Rothwell, & Scott, K.N. (Eds.), *Antarctic Security in the Twenty-First Century: Legal and Policy Perspectives* (pp. 284-306). New York: Routledge.

Scott, S.V. (2011). Ingenious and innocuous: Article IV of the Antarctic Treaty as imperialism. *Polar Journal*, 1(1), 51-52.

Secretariat of the Antarctic Treaty (2016a). *Antarctic Treaty.* http://www.ats.aq/documents/ats/treaty_original.pdf

Secretariat of the Antarctic Treaty (2016b). *Convention on the Conservation of Antarctic Marine Living Resources (CCAMLR).* http://www.ats.aq/documents/ats/ccamlr_e.pdf

Secretariat of the Antarctic Treaty (2016c). *Convention for the Conservation of Antarctic Seals (CCAS).* http://www.ats.aq/documents/recatt/Att076_e.pdf

Secretariat of the Antarctic Treaty (2016d). *Parties.* http://www.ats.aq/devas/ats_parties.aspx?lang=e

Secretariat of the Antarctic Treaty (2016e). *Protocol on Environmental Protection to the Antarctic Treaty (Madrid Protocol).* http://www.ats.aq/documents/recatt/Att006_e.pdf

Secretariat of the Antarctic Treaty (2016f). *The Antarctic Treaty Consultative Meeting.* http://www.ats.aq/e/ats_meetings_atcm.htm

Shaw, J.D., Terauds, A., Riddle, M.J., Possingham, H.P., & Chown, S.L. (2014). Antarctica's protected areas are inadequate, unrepresentative, and at risk. *PLOS Biology*, 12(6).

Sitwell, N. (2009). *Antarctic Explorer.* Chichester, UK: Ocean Explorer Maps.

Stackexchange.com (2017). *Why is the geomagnetic north pole at a different location from the magnetic north pole?* http://physics.stackexchange.com/questions/104802/why-is-the-geomagnetic-north-pole-at-a-different-location-from-the-magnetic-nort

Stokke, O.S., & Vidas, D. (Eds.) (1996). *Governing the Antarctic.* Cambridge: Cambridge University Press.

Storey, B. (2013). A keystone in a changing world. In D.W.H. Walton (Ed.), *Antarctica: Global Science from a Frozen Continent* (pp. 35-66). Cambridge University Press.

Sulikowski, C. (2013). The French connection: The role of France in the Antarctic Treaty System. In A. Brady (Ed.), *The Emerging Politics of Antarctica* (pp. 163-190). New York: Routledge.

Summerhayes, C.P. (2013). Scientists together in the cold. In D.W.H. Walton (Ed.), *Antarctica: Global Science from a Frozen Continent* (pp. 253-272). Cambridge University Press.

Thomas, W. (2014). Research agendas in climate studies: The case of the West Antarctic Ice Sheet research. *Climate Change*, 122, 299-311.

Triggs, G. (2011). The Antarctic Treaty System: A model of legal creativity and cooperation. In P.A. Berkman, Lang, M.A., Walton, D.W.H., & Young, O.R. (Eds.). *Science Diplomacy: Antarctica, Science, and the Governance of International Spaces* (pp. 39-49). Washington, DC: Smithsonian Institution Scholarly Press.

Turner, J. et al (2014). *Antarctic Climate Change and the Environment – 2014 Update.* XXXVII Antarctic Treaty Consultative Meeting, Brasilia. http://epic.awi.de/35832/1/2014_ATCM37_ip060_e.pdf

Tvedt, M.W. (2009). Patent law and bioprospecting in Antarctica. *Polar Record*, 17(1326), 1-10.

United Nations (2016a). *Agreement for the Implementation of … the Conservation and Management of Straddling Fish Stocks and Highly Migratory Fish Stocks.* http://www.un.org/depts/los/convention_agreements/conventi on_overview_fish_stocks.htm

United Nations (2016b). *Convention on the Law of the Sea.* http://www.un.org/depts/los/convention_agreements/texts/un clos/unclos_e.pdf

United Nations (2016c). *Food and Agriculture Organization. Agreement to Promote Compliance and Management Measures by Fishing Vessels on the High Seas (Article III).* http://www.fao.org/docrep/meeting/003/x3130m/X3130E00. HTM#b4

United Nations (2016d). *Food and Agriculture Organization. World's first illegal fishing treaty now in force.* http://www.fao.org/news/story/en/item/417286/icode/

United Nations (2016e). *Overview.* http://www.un.org/en/sections/about-un/overview/index.html

United Nations (2016f). *Submissions ... to the Commission on the Limits of the Continental Shelf.* http://www.un.org/depts/los/clcs_new/commission_submissions.htm

U.S. Antarctic Resource Center (2016). *Topographic Reconnaissance Maps.* U.S. Geological Survey. http://usarc.usgs.gov/drg_dload.shtml

U.S. Central Intelligence Agency (2016). *Antarctica.* World Factbook. https://www.cia.gov/library/publications/the-world-factbook/geos/ay.html

U.S. Central Intelligence Agency (2016). *Southern Ocean.* World Factbook. https://www.cia.gov/library/publications/the-world-factbook/geos/oo.html

U.S. Geological Survey (2016). *The USGS Water Science School.* https://water.usgs.gov/edu/wetstates.html

U.S. Office of the Historian (2016). *Purchase of Alaska, 1867.* https://history.state.gov/milestones/1866-1898/alaska-purchase

University of Texas (2016). *Polar Regions and Ocean Maps: Antarctic Region (Political) 2002.* http://www.lib.utexas.edu/maps/islands_oceans_poles/antarct ic_region_pol02.jpg

University of Waterloo (2008). *Interactive Map.* Canadian Space Agency. http://www.dailymail.co.uk/sciencetech/article-2729731/Antarctica-unprecedented-Most-complete-map-reveals-continent-shrinking-rapidly.html

Verbitsky, J. (2013). Titanic Part II: Tourism, uncertainty, and insecurity in Antarctica. In A. Brady (Ed.), *The Emerging Politics of Antarctica* (pp. 220-241). New York: Routledge.

Vidas, D. (1996a). The Antarctic Treaty System in the international community: An overview. In O.S. Stokke & D. Vidas (Eds.), *Governing the Antarctic* (pp. 35-60). Cambridge: Cambridge University Press.

Vidas, D. (1996b). The Antarctic Treaty System and the law of the sea: A new dimension introduced by the Protocol. In O.S. Stokke & D. Vidas (Eds.), *Governing the Antarctic* (pp. 61-90). Cambridge: Cambridge University Press.

Walton, D.W.H. (Ed.) (2013). *Antarctica: Global Science from a Frozen Continent.* Cambridge University Press.

Walton, D.W.H. (2013). Discovering the unknown continent. In D.W.H. Walton (Ed.), *Antarctica: Global Science from a Frozen Continent* (pp. 1-34). Cambridge University Press.

Whale and Dolphin Conservation (2016). *International Convention for the Regulation of Whaling.* http://us.whales.org/issues/in-depth/international-convention-for-regulation-of-whaling-icrw

The Author

Dr. Craig is an Associate Professor in the Political Science Department at Troy University in Alabama.

Dissertation

Craig, K. (1996). *Empirical Tests of Dependency Theory in the Commonwealth Caribbean* (Doctoral dissertation, University of Mississippi, 1995). Dissertation Abstracts International, 57, 01A, 426.

Books in print and on Kindle™

Craig, K. (2008). *Economics for Public Administrators: Classic European Liberalism.* ISBN-13: 978-1492130239

Craig, K. (2011). *No Representation without Taxation: Finding Middle Ground between Universal Suffrage and Absolute Rule.* ISBN-13: 978-1492167105

Craig, K. (2013). *The American Inquisition: A Dystopian State of Affairs.* ISBN-13: 978-1492789345

Craig, K. (2014). *Feminism and Socialism in Postmodern America.* ISBN-13: 978-1495257865

Journal Articles

Craig, K. (2010). Simplification: A single tax and a single entitlement. *Journal of US-China Public Administration*, 7(4), 47-53.

Craig, K. (2010). The extension of territorial waters. *US-China Law Review*, 7(5), 15-25.

Craig, K. (2010). The new world order: A deconstruction of the nation-state and a disaggregation of the mixed-political-economy. *International Journal of Public Administration*, 33(8-9), 414-420.

Craig, K. (2011). The blame game in international relations. *National Social Science Journal*, 35(2), 43-54.

Craig, K. (2012). No child left bewildered: Using phonetic English as a lingua franca. *International Journal of Business and Social Science*, 3(8), 76-82.

Craig, K. (2012). No child left behind: Teaching the metric system in US schools. *International Journal of Applied Science and Technology*, 2(4), 40-48.

Craig, K. (2013). What do the United States and India have in common (besides Indians): Enough for a strategic alliance? *Asian Social Science*, 9(2), 70-98.

Craig, K. (2013). Public policy in Central America: An empirical analysis. *Public Administration Research*, 2(2), 105-123.

Craig, K. (2015). Elementary and secondary education in America: Using induction and correlation to evaluate public policies and student outcomes. *Journal of Social Research & Policy*, 6(1), 1

Made in the USA
Monee, IL
10 August 2022